THE SPANNER EXPERIMENT

'Dalton will be recognised as one of the major British playwrights of the next decade' *Plays and Players,* May 1977

'[*Partisans*] gets its message across with some impact – a rarity in committed fringe theatre these days – and still manages to be highly entertaining' *Manchester Evening News,* October 1978

'The range of reactions . . . is beautifully observed with a knowing objectivity which is unimpaired by Mr Dalton's commitment to whatever it is he's committed to. The only thing that worried me is what will happen, when Mr Dalton is offered a residency at the National or the RSC, to Spanner?' *Guardian,* October 1978

'. . . short and sharp, with a lot of humour and some real feeling. It is a long time since I saw a piece of agit-prop that portrayed factory workers as human beings. Here we have the backsliders, the unsure, the fearful and fatalistic, the hopeful and the idealistic . . . a little gem' *Guardian,* November 1978

Ernest Dalton is a writer and member of the Neuf experimental film-makers group. He also works as a patient teacher and facilitator of health communication in medical schools and community organisations, in the UK and Chicago. He is married with a daughter and a son.

THE SPANNER EXPERIMENT

*Rediscovering two minor masterpieces
of 1970s agit-prop theatre*

ERNEST DALTON

In memory of Mum and Dad

Published in Great Britain by
Just Press
www.justpress.co.uk

British Library Cataloguing in Publication Data
A catalogue record for this book is available from the British Library
Library of Congress Cataloging in Publication Data
A catalog record for this book is available from the Library of Congress

Just Press offers books, DVDs, art works and lectures/exhibitions that
provide a platform for exchange between different generations and
interests. In areas including history, religion, theatre, health, politics,
art, poetry and fiction, we honour unsung aspects of human experience
and celebrate the unorthodox. Just Press is a non-profit project.

ISBN 978-1-907352-01-0

Design, editing, typesetting and cover design by
The Running Head Limited, Cambridge, www.therunninghead.com

Printed and bound in Great Britain by
TJ International Ltd, Padstow, Cornwall

We would like to express our thanks to John Sturrock for the use of his
photographs of North West Spanner in action.

An earlier version of the introduction appeared in the *North West
Labour History Journal*, 27, 2004, pp. 68–74.

Contents

Introduction:
The way we were...

North West Spanner was a small-scale community theatre company (five members including an administrator) that thrived from 1973/4 to 1982/3. *Just a Cog* (1976) and *Partisans* (1978) are two of the plays that were written for and performed to mainly working-class audiences during the turbulent 1970s. I am grateful to Just Press for the opportunity to publish them now, over three decades on. Looking back, it feels like a lifetime ago. The industrial and political landscape of Britain has changed fundamentally since then. During the 1970s, trade unions were core to working-class identity and survival. They were led, in the main, by a generation that had lived through the Second World War and who had been instrumental in the foundation of the Welfare State. But the pledge never to return to the mass unemployment and poverty of the 1930s was being undermined by increasing industrial decline. Britain, once the 'workshop of the world', faced an uncertain future. It was into this world that our theatre company was born. These plays give voice to the raging arguments and struggles of the time. They record our youthful enthasiasm for a better tomorrow.

We performed sixty to eighty main shows a year, and when we got into our stride we were a regular fixture at Manchester community, political and trade union events for ten years, but we also toured to other regions of England and Scotland. What follows is a personal memoir of the time I wrote and performed in these plays, a re-engagement with the young man I was.

In 1973 I was 21 years old and full of fire. All I knew were the experiences of growing up on a council estate in west London in a large family, headed by a Communist father and a Catholic mother. Any artistic aspiration I had was formed by a desperate need to escape from the destiny of manual work that was mapped out for me. It was always a class thing. Knowing your place and where you came from. Somehow, and this bit remains a mystery, I found myself, after originally leaving school at 15, hitch-hiking up to Manchester in the autumn of 1972 to go to university. By that time I had already been at two further education establishments and had got the basic entrance requirements for a degree course.

That first term at Manchester we occupied the administration block and held the Vice-Chancellor to ransom over our demands for an alternative curriculum. After the Miners' Strike of 1972 and the Three Day Week this student stuff seemed a piece of cake. I thought I had digested everything that you needed to know about class war, and young as I was often found myself in the front line. I wasn't alone in believing the old order was crumbling and now was our chance to go in for the kill. For we are many and they are few. These thoughts were the backdrop to my discussions about Trotsky, Lenin, Marx and Engels and the need to build an independent working-class organisation not just in itself but for itself. At that moment I might have been kipping on the floor of comrades in Crumpsall but one more push and . . .

Perhaps I always was sensitive and had a personal need to self-express rather than accept learning. I certainly felt out of place both at university and, if I am honest, in Manchester. I was a long way from my roots, and as I acclimatised in those first months I began to look around me. This was Manchester before they cleaned the Victorian grime off the stone buildings. A Utopian Salford might have arisen on the new Ellor Street estate but the semi-derelict rows of terraces were still full of families in conditions not much changed from the 1930s. Oh, they were coming down soon, but I'll never forget the lives that confronted me in Lower Broughton.

It was culture shock. I might have ideas about the coming revolution, but here now, then, the degradation of thousands at the bottom of the heap, still having to shit in outside toilets while paying the council rent, called for a more immediate response.

I met my life-long collaborator and partner Penny Morris walking across Sussex Street, Lower Broughton. I remember she was wearing rainbow-coloured Wellington boots and a bright yellow three-quarter-length coat and with her blonde hair she appeared a benign inter-galactic visitor. She was a member of Inroads, a community action group of York University graduates based in Lower Broughton. Their mission was to involve the community in education through play.

It took me a while to understand this approach. They lived as a proto-commune, shared breakfast from large buckets of wholesale muesli and were devising programmes of innovative activities that drew large support from the families amongst whom they lived. Inroads was one of a number of pioneering national groups that gave birth to the community arts movement. In today's parlance, a kind of third way. This was action that not only changed people's minds but also their relationships and direct physical environment. These were the days before the incorporation of the movement into the fabric of local authority management. I was hooked.

Inroads had as part of its work a kind of street performance troupe. When I encountered them they had just begun a show called *The Rents Play*. This was a series of funny sketches opposing the then outrageous increase of council rents by 50 pence a week. It was that long ago. The show was performed to tenants' associations around Manchester and Salford, and was often instrumental in bringing isolated tenants together to form their own organisation.

I joined the group and found myself. Although wearing a papier-mâché mask of Edward Heath (we still have that) and being funny might have seemed a long way from Marx's *Grundrisse*, it was the first time I had real fun in political activity. Definitely more Max Wall than Wolfe Tone.

It wasn't a long apprenticeship but soon the idea of North West Spanner was born. We formed a more independent part of Inroads to concentrate solely on writing and performing plays that sprang from issues within the local community, only now that community had stretched to span all of Manchester and the North West. 'Spanner' because it was a work tool, and work rather than homes would be our focus. This first Spanner group's members were Penny, me, Jon Blishen, Sharon Nassaur, Gill Ingel and Tierl Thompson.

There was a nurses' strike in 1973 and we wrote *H.M.S.N.H.S.*, a skit on nurses' pay and conditions and the sinking health service, and performed it to picket lines in their support. There quickly followed another mainly agit-prop piece called *Free the Shrewsbury 24* about a group of building workers who were being prosecuted for daring to form a trade union. I learnt a lot about the flexibility needed when writing and performing these issue-based sketches. Something that really pissed me off at the time was that we kept having to change the title of the Shrewsbury play. The police, no doubt in concert with the Building Employers' Federation and the Official Solicitor, kept dropping charges against some of the 24. What began as *Free the 24* soon went down to *Free the 18, Free the 10, Free the 5 . . . 4 . . .* finally, (and boy was I pleased after all our hard work they didn't let them all off) *Free the Shrewsbury 2*. Des Warren and the now famous star of stage and screen Ricky Tomlinson were eventually stitched up and banged up. Just as well because we had a long list of building sites booked to tour. Sorry, Des. It probably made Ricky though.

What a time . . . Everything seemed possible and the really miraculous thing to me wasn't only the encouragement and support we got from audiences, Trotskyist organisers, myriad wings of the Labour Party and trade union officials, but the memory of a visionary, middle-class, middle-aged, woman employee of the now defunct Greater Manchester Council. She came to see us perform this show in a building site canteen on Deansgate and, being won over by our energy, commitment and humour, supported our efforts to get a grant from the GMC to buy a van. It says something about the narrow, conformist opportunities available to the young today that of all the events written about in this introduction, this fact remains the most unbelievable to me.

By then I felt fervently that theatre, performance, opening your mouth and letting the truth out, would inspire the disaffected downtrodden masses, often in bitter struggle with their employers, to rise up and liberate themselves. Our work could have an impact far beyond the meagre resources that fuelled it.

We needed to become more professional. There were anteced-ents. Although Spanner had sprung from a local community, and would always be proud of that authority and seek to stay close and involved where we lived and worked, none of us had any training. We looked to other theatre groups like Claire and Roland Mul-doon's CAST, also 7:84, Belt and Braces and Red Ladder, as well as a host of other small scale, weird and wonderful theatre compa-nies springing up. Don't ask me to describe what Forkbeard Fantasy Theatre thought they were doing but I was always bowled over by Welfare State, an extraordinary performance art group who called themselves engineers of the imagination.

After our first burst of independent activity, the time came to have a break. Penny and I and Jon Blishen got jobs in hospitals to earn some money and think what we might do next. The other members of this first group moved on and off. The Shrewsbury play was still in demand, they were still in jail. While working at Tame-side General Hospital, Manchester, we put in an application to the Arts Council to found a full-time theatre company – half-subsidised by our local arts council, North West Arts. Older and wiser by this time at 23, I thought: what did we have to lose? The money would enable us to live on a minimum wage and, as I then thought, do proper plays, i.e. ones that lasted longer than 25 minutes.

I was working as a hospital theatre porter, wheeling all sorts, from the shirkers (painter, in-growing toe-nail, off work six weeks on pay) to the heartbreaking (a young mother facing major abdominal surgery), out of the wards to the knife, when I made a call to find out if we'd got the grant. I think it was after I'd dropped off one par-ticularly distressing patient and my mind was elsewhere. The posh lady asked me to wait while she looked down a list. I was in the cor-ridor on the public phone in my green theatre garb when she said, perfunctorily, yes. I'm not sure if it was the constant need to switch off from emotional reaction in work or I couldn't take in the yes bit, but I then asked curtly, 'When do we get the money?' Reality began to sink in fast: 'You will have to fill in some forms . . .'

At the time we were living in Mossley, and the idea of being able to leave work and do political theatre seemed incongruous. We were so lucky, but I never questioned it. Next day, I rang from the same corridor and poached Carlos Guarita (who went on to become a fine photojournalist) from Red Ladder. Carlos was born in London to Portuguese parents near where I grew up. He became a life-long friend after I rescued him. That's not fair, but I am painting a picture here. Carlos is an artist, but his ability to project character and to graft was part of the foundation of Spanner. He made our portable performing backdrop that lasted ten years. He only stayed a year and then he went and joined the Portuguese revolution of 1974. I ask you, what an excuse. That first twelve months established us.

A key member, and God knows how she did it while raising a young family, was Maureen Ramsey. She became our administrator, and, along with Penny, did all the paperwork. And there was enough of that. Maureen fixed all the bookings, finding and persuading contacts and then chasing them to set up the place and the crowd; and in later years, she would book rooms, put up posters, sell tickets, turn up. We always said 'the audience is the other half of our plays', and her efforts got them there.

Spanner proper began with the arrival of Newman Smith and Elsie Hallsworth. They were chalk and cheese. Newman, a railwayman with piercing wit, joined us after I convinced him of the importance of a chance to establish a true working class, popular theatre. I think he was drunk at the time. And Elsie was a mature mill worker from Ashton-under-Lyne. She was not only beautiful but also conveyed a sincerity and truthfulness that inspired me to write our first longer play, *Winding Up*. But that came later.

Safety First or Last? was a 25-minute sketch about exactly what it says on the tin. Manual work is often highly dangerous and can kill you. The interests of the employers are diametrically opposed to those of the workforce. We needed a play that would put that unambiguous message across. We wanted to perform to factories, so it had to be short, fast, funny and be able to be performed anywhere: inside the gates, outside the gates, in the canteen. It featured the Indestructible Workman (irony), the body clocks (effects of shift-work) and Bruce 'Life is the name of the game' Fosdyke and the Generation Game. It ended with us lining up and saying the immortal words 'Is it safety first for you and your family or safety last for your boss and his profits?'

It usually went down a storm and was performed everywhere: from Salford Dry Docks to Govan Shipyards. In those years the unions had clout. And they exercised it. Often we were invited into places by shop steward committees who had booked us under the noses of the management as a non-controversial event, to raise the issue of safety. In Oldham the whole workforce was given half an hour off work to assemble in the canteen and watch the show. Their roars of approval as the show went on drowned the embarrassment of bosses sitting at the back. But the look of contempt on some of the management's faces as we got to those final words . . . if we'd have been in Chile we'd have been shot. I think it was this play that led to us having a spot of bother with the authorities later. That embarrassment took a while to ferment into revenge, but when it did, it led to a national showdown.

Meanwhile we had hired from Tameside Council the top half of the old St Peter's School in Ashton-under-Lyne. The West End was an area undergoing its own regeneration. It had a young Community Centre and some great local activists. They generously welcomed us to the area and we premiered our plays at the Centre for years.

All around us were the remnants of the once formidable Lancashire textile industry. King Cotton was threadbare in 1975, and the mills that were still going were under threat of closure throughout the North West. The way I saw it then, it was a cut and dried story. Big conglomerates were asset stripping and throwing lives and communities on the scrapheap. Courtaulds, a famous name, became infamous for this. With Elsie Hallsworth as the central character, I wrote *Winding Up*. Elsie had worked in the local mills for years; a scene that I hope will stand the test of time is where she sits in Trafalgar Square, having gone down to London to protest about the closure of her mill, and sings a song that was written by her husband, David. It used to bring a tear to my eye every time she sang it. Mournful yet inspirational, it was the highlight of a play that interspersed the story of mill workers fighting mill closure with agit-prop scenes depicting the carving up of the textile industry in the face of cheap imports.

Granada Television approached us as we were about to perform the play at a rare sit-in at the Adelphi Mill in Bollington, Cheshire. The film of our performance and their action made it on to the airwaves. How times have changed. It was memorable. A contemporary play in every sense of the word, in those days it did not seem so unusual.

With this rich experience behind us, our confidence grew. We began to take the show to audiences outside the North West. Under pressure from the Arts Council to tour nationally to justify their grant, we arranged some performances in arts venues as well as to our bread and butter audiences in factories, community centres and trades clubs. Somehow *Winding Up* was booked into the Institute of Contemporary Arts in London. It was one of the first times that members of the Arts Council saw our work, the venue being a short hop from their headquarters in Piccadilly. It went down like a lead balloon, not least because during the final scene I lost my lines and just stood there frozen. Remembering it now, I see a sea of shocked faces with my heart about to burst.

After the show I quickly went on the attack about the iniquity of arts funding and how my lost lines were a symptom of this. I wish I was 23 again and could put up a similar defence. But we got through it, and whatever their view of *Winding Up*, it had to be mediated by the report of a member of the drama panel – Mike Leigh, God bless him. He was then the rising writer of *Abigail's Party*. He saw us doing the Safety play to an audience of nurses at Hammersmith Hospital and was kind, or just seditious in his own way.

The Safety play was usually a workplace, lunchtime show, a loss leader for contacts and access to the trade union movement generally. As we began to find our form, the idea began to grow, along with our confidence, that we could also draw in to an evening venue an audience who had never thought before of attending a play.

Manchester had a famed engineering past. John Tocker, the legendary leader of the engineering union AUEW, was still active, and the legacy of the Manchester day work agreement still resounded in the fears of the Engineering Employers' Federation. It was increasingly a sign of the times that, with a fragile Labour government, the employers – particularly the aging captains of engineering – started to encroach into union territory. There was a sense that Britain Ltd was on the ropes in manufacturing. The sea change throughout all sectors of industry was that old practices – and then that meant the idea of unions at all – would drag the country into the economic abyss. A century of union struggle for a decent standard of living and the right to work was being targeted as the problem.

The far Left, in the shape of the Trotskyite groups like the International Socialists (to become the Socialist Workers Party, or SWP) and the Socialist Labour League, as well as the Militant faction in the Labour Party, were trying to point the finger at the big 'C' of Capitalism while stirring it at grassroots level. I shared the view of many of my SWP friends about the need to get from the shop floor to the revolutionary revenge squads as quickly as possible, but I think it was about this time that I began to feel my ideas were more potent than any dead Russian's or any dead anybody's.

I shared a lot with these comrades and friends, including fighting in the streets against the National Front sometimes, but listening to those groups' leaders often made me seethe. Out would come the pre-war pretext that what was happening in Madrid and Macau, Manchester or Mossley was due to the inevitability of the collapse of capitalism as foretold by the prophets. All you had to do was repeat it often enough to poor, cloth-capped clod-heads and they too would move from no idea to their idea. When anyone with any brains could see that what ordinary British working-class people needed were champions of their own.

Eccles was a long way from Macau, but in the summer of 1976 at Automat, a small engineering firm, the workforce with an appropriate sense of history decided they should seek union recognition. Now, at any time in the previous hundred years this would have been taken at face value. Practically irritating to half a dozen managers as it would have been, this idea of belonging to a trade union was hardly the stuff of social breakdown. In fact, from my reading of the history of the making of the working class, social order and responsibility grew from precisely this impetus. So why did this tuppenny-halfpenny firm hold fast against it?

Well, there is always a version of history that never finds its way between hard covers. Defeated voices rarely get a book deal, academic or not, but some say that behind the short walls of a small factory big names talked of making a stand. Sadly, they were not on the union side. I heard rumours that a right-wing, semi-underground, national organisation called Trumid (I forget what the name stood for) bolstered a naïve management into trying to breach the fortress that was once the engineering union in Manchester. To test the resolve and organising capability of the local AUEW, and rather than risk the order list of a major manufacturer, the better battleground was Automat. So the die was cast and negotiation soon became confrontation. As ever, the workers, those who stood up for the right to join a trade union, ended up outside the gates in a protracted dispute.

Our response was our next play, *Just a Cog*. This followed *Winding Up* in terms of length (just under an hour), but dropped the more agit-prop scenes in favour of creating four very individual characters, in a similar factory to Automat, who were asked to support their dispute. Using these characters I tried to explore the fears, anxieties and tensions within the local union movement about how to respond to this challenge to union power, at a time when many felt they could be next to lose their jobs. It also marked the beginning of my growing writing confidence. I felt I knew people better, and in Elsie, Newman, Penny and myself, had performers who carried credibility and power. My character was a cockney jack-the-lad who was more interested in football than politics, but who was slowly won over by the seriousness of his workmates. Elsie played an older union official who had seen it all but was tired and had been let down by her workforce in struggle before. Newman was the earnest class fighter with a vicious streak, and Penny tried to get us to show solidarity.

This airing of the difficulties faced on the shop floor when asked for support did not always meet with the approval of union officials, who worried we might put people off. This became Spanner's signature. Don't be frightened to tell it how it is. We felt this gave our work its strength. We would need to call on this strength for our-selves soon enough. We performed the play all over Manchester and beyond, to benefits in support of Automat and, of course, for the strikers themselves. I hope it boosted their spirits. It would be nice to write that it had a happy ending: the big union battalions rode over the hill and justice prevailed. They didn't, it didn't; with hind-sight it was a taste of future things to come – ominously, for us too.

The monarchy never featured as much of a political target for me. Apart from the odd reference to passing out carpets from Buck-ingham Palace come the revolution, I've always thought it was an institution beyond my interest. But 1977 was Silver Jubilee year and after Spanner's previous years as a burgeoning theatre of the people, how could we ignore this institution's faux embrace? My dad's con-tempt for all aristocracy was indoctrinated into me so much that by the age of 10 I was being singled out for caning by the nuns in my primary school for declaring, in history lessons, that after the French Revolution and the blue bloods' heads had rolled, the Industrial Revolution in Britain was a last ditch attempt by a desper-ate aristocracy to give the middle classes something to keep their minds occupied.

The Small Truth of Kings was a light-hearted series of sketches, which seem now to contain some of the most profound things I wrote. The 'small truth' simply being the extraordinary staying power of the monarchy's hold on popular imagination. My pierc-ing social commentary even now is blunted describing why this is. The key metaphor I chose to illustrate the power of this hold was to liken it to a family's favourite wardrobe. Think about it, and I did. So I sawed a wardrobe in half and that was the stage setting for dis-located conversations between members of a family about loss and identity. I think I was suffering inner turmoil at the time. But we made a strong pitch at social analysis nonetheless. It was during that show that I would slice copies of the newspaper up with a double-edged Wilkinson Sword old-fashioned razor blade, then rotate it – to the gasps of audiences – in my mouth. One proletarian fan said this was the best thing I'd ever done.

1977 was a year to remember. If I thought we were on the cutting edge of contemporary culture, experimenting with what and how things could be said, nothing prepared me for waking up one morning at a friend's house in Salford to be confronted by a green-haired Howard Devoto making coffee. Punk rock was erupting around us. Newman came in late to rehearsal that day humming 'God save the Queen, the fascist regime,' saying he'd seen Siouxsie and the Banshees the night before in some dive off Manchester's Oxford Street and their energy blew him away. I was annoyed because it took a while for him to settle down to repeating my freshly written dialogue, which, I was certain, would change lives if spoken with the right amount of passion. His passion seemed focused elsewhere that day.

Although Spanner felt part of some loose alternative to the mainstream, throughout Manchester events and people were springing up who confirmed that we were from a very different mould of dissent. We had made close ties with John Crumpton and the Manchester Film and Video Workshop and other community arts groups, but it was hard not to reflect that times were a-changing and we needed to find some way to respond. Our audiences were usually much older than the youth rebellion troops assembling around the proto-Haciendas. When I first heard the Buzzcocks I thought they should change their name. And if I thought we would be eclipsed by these young cultural anarchists, slow-burn news reached us that summer that would propel our group to the top of the Manchester scandal chart. Elsie, perhaps realising she'd done enough, left and went to work in a steady job with a union. Chris Tupman joined, our very own scouse punk who had worked with the children's group Inroads in Lower Broughton.

Our yearly survival was dependent on receiving grants from the Arts Council and North West Arts. This latter organisation was staffed by well meaning and supportive individuals who, while not always seeing the point of what we were trying to do, accepted that by any standard we deserved some funding, playing to audiences who otherwise didn't go to the theatre and whose interests were under-represented in the arts. I think the phrase used to describe us was experimental theatre. The criteria for funding were clear and we obviously did what we said we did and were proud of it. This did not stop a local Tory councillor, a member of the extreme National Association for Freedom (NAF), successfully calling at the North West Arts Board for our grant to be blocked, with an official investation into our 'aims and ideals'. He claimed our plays cried 'blood, blood, we want blood on the streets!' He obviously hadn't seen them, but his witch-hunt gathered some tempo. Roland Muldoon of CAST reminded us about the American McCarthyite battles, and urged us to refuse any cooperation with political interference. This emboldened North West Arts and the Arts Council, the overseers of our fitness for a grant, to do the same. The blatant attempt at political censorship thrust Spanner into the media spotlight nationwide. Penny called a conference against political censorship, and went head to head with the NAF councillor on local television, defending the right to free expression. We became headline news in *The Stage* newspaper, a question was asked in the House of Commons and we were heartened by support from a wide cross-section of the arts world. This culminated with the General Secreatary of the Arts Council, Roy Shaw, reaffirming that theatre companies were funded only on the basis of their artistic merit, and our grant was reinstated. But it was obvious our cards were now marked.

We had reached the limit of what it was possible to do under state patronage. Ultimately, and this took some time, funding organisations learnt other methods to control the kind of creativity they were prepared to sponsor.

Sensing time was running out helped produce our best work. 1977 ended with us fighting for survival and me writing *Out of Control*. This play was about the Windscale (now Sellafield) nuclear reprocessing plant and the dangers of radiation. It was the beginning of the intense concern about the proposed expansion of this facility and some of the contradictions it imposed on the workforce there. We performed it in Workington, close to the site. I remember it provoked fierce debate afterwards between early green activists and union officials who saw the plant as a vital part of the area's economic survival. It was moving too, as there were some parents at the show who maintained that Windscale was responsible for their children's birth defects – a charge hotly denied by cornered union representatives.

Some of the humour in the show fell flat as members of the audience began to get nervous about what we might say next. A few expressed their concern afterwards that even being at the performance might get back to management and go against them at work. I thought this was a bit paranoid until the next day, when we arrived at the small town closest to the plant. While we were setting up and were distracted, two blokes wearing smart suits burst into the hall and scooped up copies of an alternative report about the plant that we used to distribute after the show. They ran out, got into a waiting car and sped out of the car park, tyres screeching. Very strange.

Meanwhile, Jim Callaghan's minority Labour government were hanging on to power. In 1978 I remember riding a white horse, dressed as Callaghan, at the Mayday celebrations of Stockport Trades Council. What was that about?

That summer I wrote *Partisans*. This 50-minute play became my favourite and I think it is the best-written thing I did. By this time we had the four people and hardboard stagecraft down to a T. Although set in a small engineering factory in Manchester again, the play was loosely about the takeover by Peugeot, the French car manufacturer, of parts of the ailing Rootes/Chrysler empire. I felt freest writing this play, and it distilled in character and situation many of the themes explored in the past by Spanner. At times surreal, heartfelt and inspiring, it took on the end logic of class struggle.

It starts with the occupation of the factory by the four characters: Ferry (me), as in 'ferry 'cross the Mersey, Mersey Tunnel, mouth as wide as', a one-time militant on anti-depressants, and Mole (Chris Tupman), so named because, although he left the factory every night by the main gate, he spent as much time as he could digging a tunnel out of the factory from behind his hardboard lathe. Symbolism, that. There was also Birdman (Newman Smith), recently released from Her Majesty's Pleasure in Walton. An edgy piece of work, him. And, finally, Hammer (Penny), who spends the play corralling us to act as one mind and out of joint interest. No easy job.

We took this show all over the country and had some memorable highs and lows. We had built up a trade union fan base in the Black Country of all places, and we were big in Dudley. Our venues were packed out with people confident they would have a good time. They did and we did. Whether it was the surrealism that smacked of self-indulgence, or the power of my character's misanthropic, greedy worker speech with me fantasising about eating old age pensioners clutching tins of salmon, I don't know, but we bombed in Preston.

Perhaps it was the emotional extremes we continually experienced which finally took a personal toll on us. *Partisans* had been our most successful play, and by this time even the newspaper critics praised us, but it was not enough to hold the group together.

Newman and Chris left in the summer of 1979. Earlier, what came to be known as the winter of discontent bled into the irresistible rise of Maggie Thatcher. The shock we felt as the reality of the change in the national political landscape sank in was one I do not want to experience again. The feelings of my political generation's defeat could not be avoided. What the hell could we do or say now? For ten years I thought we were building something, going somewhere. When the idea emerged for a Right to Work march from Lands End to John O'Groats, I felt like doing myself in.

The thing that saved me was the Rock against Racism concert in Platt Fields in south Manchester. Being one of the compères gave me my first taste of communication to the masses. I know they were mostly there to hear the bands – Aswad, Graham Parker and the Rumour et al. – and everyone seemed 10 years old, but if nothing else we had the Nazis on the run. I made one or two tremendously powerful points to the throng. They thronged back with two rows of punks gobbing in unison at my evening-dress-be-suited self. I heard afterwards in some disbelief that this constituted approval in their orbit. At the back of my mind was the thought we were still some distance from a shared understanding of the relationship between the structure and superstructure that Marx so eloquently wrote about when denouncing Hegelian dialectic.

In haste, we agreed to join forces with CAST theatre group from London and tour a production of the American writer Clifford Odets' play *Waiting for Lefty*. This classic of American labour theatre, a rabble-rousing tour de force about the need to stand up and fight for union rights, had audiences used to Spanner's own house style bemused and disappointed. It was a desperate clutching at straws and when, after its national tour, I ended up in an isolation hospital suffering from viral meningitis, I thought it served me right. For two weeks the only visitors I had were made to wear white coats and face masks to prevent the spread of infection. I had time, for the first time, to reflect on the decade and all it meant. Historical perspective is elusive.

I surfaced from isolation, writing and performing an autobiographical one-man show *I, a Mongrel*. All I felt I could do was to begin to speak personally to audiences, to try and make sense of all that had gone before. International tensions began to reach boiling point and people feared nuclear war. The Conservative government got busy cementing their position of power that would last the next 18 years. Generations would grow up knowing nothing of what had gone on in the decade before 1979.

Spanner did do a couple more plays into the 1980s. My last written one was *I Owe My Soul to the Company Store*, about new technology and old working practices. I was leaking desperation by that time. *Symptoms of Unhealthy Patience* was our last play, led by Penny and performed by an all-women group (Penny, Elsie, Kirsten Baker and Sue Power) to some of our old audiences and new health service ones. Its themes – exploring health, relationships and personal stories – grew into the work Spanner has undertaken since that time in medical education.

The 1970s have become a lost decade. Fashion may have rekindled affection for flared trousers, zig-zag wallpaper and the lava lamp, but the politics of that time remain obscure to most. Ironically, at the time of writing this there is war, worldwide recession and a threat of the collapse of capitalism. Well, arrivederci and Lotto Continua (not a lotta!).

Just a Cog

The play is set at MEL Engineering Ltd (MEL's) in Manchester, where the news of a strike over union recognition at Automat, another local engineering company, has just begun. The year is 1976, when it was written.

Characters

PETE, 25: Pete's father is dead, his mother cleans at the hospital. He served his time at MEL's and has worked there now for almost ten years. His political views come from being in the union on the shop floor. He is suspicious of union leadership both in his own union and others. Unmarried, he plays football in the same team as John. Born and bred in Longsight, Manchester, but now lives in Stockport. He was at one time considered for a place at Ruskin College but failed to take it up.

PAT, 26: Pat is a semi-skilled engineering worker who was lucky to get a job at MEL's after having two kids. She resents her husband, Tom, who works shifts on Greater Manchester Transport buses; she is unhappy at home with the pressure of kids and a husband who ignores her. At work she likes the friendship of fellow workers. Basically she's thoughtful, at times piercing the conversations on any topic with a clarity that even John admires. Her main friend is Mary, the older union woman. She obviously sees Mary as a woman who has broken down many of the restrictions she feels.

Being under the wing of Mary, she's pro the union in a pragmatic way. Her friend Barbara works at Automat. It's Pat who brings the question of Automat into the factory.

JOHN, 25: John has worked at MEL's for four years. Left London when he finished his apprenticeship and moved to Manchester to support Manchester United. That sums up John. The joker of the factory, basically he's out for number one. But as the Joker he dances rather than sits on the fence.

MARY, 50: Mary has fought all her life for the working classes, as she sees it. She is well known in the local branch of the Amalgamated Union of Engineering Workers. Her husband died 15 years ago. Since then her life has been devoted to the union and to her work. It shows. Rarely does she question the union leadership, seeing the union as something you can't afford to challenge.

REPORTER: a cameo of a red-top journalist creating the truth to be told.

Scene 1

(On stage: A large cog-shaped backdrop with curtains in the centre. We are at MEL's Engineering. Up stage left there is a notice board. From behind the curtain, struggling to get through, JOHN enters carrying an 8-foot-long spanner-shaped seat. He steps out cautiously, looking from side to side.)

JOHN (to audience): It's surprising what you can get up to at work really, isn't it? If you see the security guard coming, give me a shout will you? Take this for instance. (Points to spanner.) I've been making it as a foreigner in the Fabrication Shop in my dinner hours over the last few weeks. My mate Ged wants it for his garden. It's a kind of garden seat cum ... (Looks at spanner.) ... cum 8-foot spanner. I arrived at work a bit early this morning to try and get it past the night guards when they changed shifts. But I got stopped as I came by Personnel. Horace, who cleans early morning at MEL's, kept me talking. He said he wants one. So I missed my chance. God knows how I can get it out now. Blimey, here comes Bailey, the boss! (*Shouts into distance.*) Morning Mr Bailey! (*Back to audience.*) He's a two-faced sod. One of the Knutsford jet set – all mouth and shiny suit backside. Pete, he's a shop steward here at MEL's, said he went in to see him the other day. Bailey bent down in front of him and Pete said he saw his reflection in Bailey's backside, looming up at him. Some position for negotiation, that. Christ, they'll all be here in a minute. I'll just have to leave it here. (*He sets spanner down stage opposite notice board.*)

(PETE *enters from side of stage.*)

PETE: What are you doing here at this time? It's not like you to be here before 7.30.

JOHN: I had to come in a bit early to try to get that bloody spanner out past Sweeney and his desperadoes on the gates.

PETE: I told you before you started making it you'd never get it out.

JOHN: But there's 25 quid there. Tell you what, give me a hand to get it out and I'll give you a fiver.

PETE: Just leave it and we'll try and think of a way to get it through the gates. You cockneys are all the same. Come on, that new supervisor's on our section this morning.

(PETE *exits.*)

JOHN (*to audience again*): That's Pete, he's not a bad lad, a bit of a hothead though, union mad. Bailey was telling me he's a troublemaker, very left wing. Of course, as a regular Catholic Club member myself, I don't hold with too much of this union talk. Don't get me wrong, I'm a Section One man in the AUEW. It's just you've got to give and take, and I'm a moderate. Mind you, Pete's the best outside left our works team ever had. Outside left . . . yes, that'll be Pete.

(*PAT enters and crosses stage.*)

PAT: Still skiving, John?

JOHN: That's just like Pat. Always has a nice word for me first thing in the morning. Hard-faced she is, a bit of a dark horse. You have to be careful what you say to her, she's a bit touchy. (*MARY enters.*) Morning, Mary.

MARY: What are you up to now? What's that?

JOHN: You've probably never seen a precision tool like this before. We craftsmen call it a spanner.

MARY: You could have fooled me. It looks more like a garden seat.

(*MARY exits.*)

JOHN (*to audience*): That's Mary down to a T, always awkward. She's been a shop steward here for donkey's years. And talk! I bet she could talk at you for five solid minutes! She really gets my goat. Rarely a day goes by without me and her having a row over something or other. The union says this, union says that. You'd think she works for the union, not MEL Engineering. No wonder the country's in crisis, with people like her in industry. Suppose I'd better go and show willing. And if the security guard comes this way, tell him you haven't seen me. Yes, it's people like me that have to get the economy back on its feet. Is that the time? Hey, Pete, are we having a brew this morning or what? (*Sings.*) 'Faith of our fathers, holy faith . . .' (*Exits.*)

(*Enter MARY and PETE.*)

PETE: What the hell is all this about? (*Holds up papers.*) That new supervisor says that Work Study is coming down to my station on Monday. It's the first I've heard about it.

MARY: I've seen Jack and some of the other stewards and they want us to get together after Wednesday's Branch meeting.

PETE: I thought after the fiasco with that firm of consultants management had cooled off the idea.

MARY: Open your eyes, Pete, they're just biding their time. Don't you worry, we'll work out something on Wednesday.

(*Enter* PAT.)

PAT: If I have to go through another morning like this, I'll stick that Carter woman's head in the press.

PETE: Been breathing down your neck again?

PAT: I had 40 per cent scrap, or so she said.

MARY: I'll have a word with her.

(*Enter* JOHN, *looking back over shoulder.*)

JOHN: Anyone heard what's going on down the road? There's a load of police down there.

PAT: That'll be Automat's.

PETE: What's happened?

PAT: Barbara works there, they're on strike.

JOHN: Another one. The country can't take it. I suppose they're out for more money.

PETE: Give it a rest, will you.

PAT: She said it's about getting the union recognised by management.

JOHN: Why's that? Is it wearing camouflage at the moment? . . . Cup of tea anyone? (*He exits.*)

MARY: Take your time making it.

PETE: I heard they were trying to get a meeting with management for months.

MARY: We'll see what support we can give them at the Branch on Wednesday.

PETE: Ask your friend what kind of support they need, Pat. It's only a tin pot firm, it can't hold out long against the AEU, but if they need anything . . . *(He arranges papers on notice board.)*

PAT: I think Barbara's a bit frightened by the whole thing. It's the first time she's joined a union, and now this has happened. Some of her mates at work didn't join, and they're still working. Says she can't get used to picketing.

MARY: I suppose they think joining the union means the sack. Tell her not to worry. It's been twenty years since my first picket line. I still remember it. It was in January, freezing it was. We were out for eight weeks, that was when I was still working for Vickers, just after the war. It might have been hard, but after we won, those eight weeks seemed like eight hours. We had a victory party in the canteen.

PAT: Funny you talking about the war, Automat's boss is called Chamberlain.

MARY: Chamberlain, there was a man. 'Peace in our time', then five years of butchery.

PETE: More like piece work in our time.

MARY: My first husband Bill was killed in France. I only knew him for 12 months before he was called up.

PAT: You married again?

MARY: Yes, Jim. He was an engineer, died of cancer, 15 years ago. After that I spent most of my time married to South Manchester AUEW Branch.

(In comes JOHN pushing a 4-foot-square picture of a large cup on stage. He sets it to one side.)

JOHN: Tea up!

PETE: Not another one of your foreigners!

JOHN: No, Work Study has just finished in the canteen. After three weeks of watching Mabel washing up 400 cups a day, they thought it would be more efficient to make one big cup and give everyone a straw . . .

(JOHN *goes to hand out straws;* PAT *and* MARY *walk off.*)

JOHN (*to them*): You can't stop technological progress you know. (*To* PETE.) What's up with those two? Pat going on again about 'what a bastard' her husband's like?

PETE: Can't you take anything seriously, just for once?

JOHN: What?

PETE: Automat.

JOHN: Well, why are they looking so glum? They're not on strike, are they?

PETE: I don't know why I bother with you sometimes.

JOHN: Because you love me . . . and I'm the best centre half in the Northern Works Premier League. Listen, are you coming training tonight?

PETE: No, I said I'd meet Ted and some of the others in the pub tonight for a chat about the District elections coming up.

JOHN: You surprise me, Pete, you really do. Where's your loyalty?

PETE: Firmly on the shop floor.

JOHN: Exactly. You're always going on about being well organised, but unless you come training regularly how are we ever going to get our team organised?

PETE: Don't you think about anything but football?

JOHN: Of course I do, but you don't come into my erotic fantasies . . . much. What's the point of worrying about these elections anyway, they're just careerists.

PETE: That's why it's important to make sure a careerist isn't elected.

JOHN: You lose me sometimes. Why not just be honest and say it's because you want one of your left winger mates elected as opposed to what you call a right winger.

PETE: I am being honest. I want a democratic union, and one way to ensure it is democratic is by getting officials elected who we know we can trust.

JOHN: Know you can control.

PETE: I've no illusions in the officials, John. When it comes down to it, the power of the union doesn't lie in AUEW House on the Crescent. It's in every engineering shop in Manchester. But it's better to have blokes who are on our side and don't lick the boss's arse.

JOHN: Now you're talking politics.

PETE: That's what it's all about. My father used to work in Hampton Chemicals in the Park.

JOHN: We've a match with them in two weeks.

PETE: His chest got so bad he couldn't walk to the bus stop in the morning without resting for ten minutes to catch his breath. The doctors said it was smoking that killed him. I bet the asbestos he was working with for 15 years didn't help. Now there's all this fuss about it and safety regulations. But it can't help him.

JOHN: This is getting a bit depressing. Want another cup of tea? Have a straw.

PETE: Ah, Work Study. I forgot they want to come to our section on Monday.

JOHN: We'd better prepare ourselves. If an example of their work is the canteen, they'll have all of us working on a 40-foot lathe by the end of the month.

(*They exit.*)

(*Enter* MARY *and* PAT.)

MARY: There is a lot of scrap here, Pat.

PAT: It's the machine, then. I can't do any better.

MARY: Are you feeling all right?

PAT: How did you manage on your own without settling down again with someone?

MARY: It wasn't a choice at the time. I just never met another man I felt I could marry after Jim. Two dead husbands were quite enough.

PAT: You never had kids?

MARY: Jim and me wanted to, but ...

PAT: I envy you.

MARY: Who minds yours?

PAT: Mum takes the youngest and picks Gary up from school. God knows what I'd do if she didn't look after them. The council's stopped that nursery opening. Mum was looking forward to having some time for herself. I feel guilty dumping the little one on her. I've a good mind to take that kid round to our local friendly councillor, let him look after her. If they voted for the nursery not to open, then let them mind the kids.

MARY: What does your husband say?

PAT: 'I told you not to go to work in the first place' is what he says.

MARY: He works on the buses, doesn't he?

PAT: Yes, works and lives on them, with his shifts. I haven't had a proper conversation with him for the last six weeks. And when we do talk, or rather when we argue, he blames me for being at work. It's not just for pin money. We need my wages to keep our heads above water. And when I wasn't working I nearly went mad stuck in the house all day.

MARY: Don't let it get you down, you've got your whole life in front of you.

PAT: If it's the same as it is now I don't want it.

(*PETE enters with a notice for the board.*)

PETE: I see the phantom drawing pin snatcher is still at large. I bet it's the new supervisor, Micrometer Harry. Are you going to see your friend Barbara tonight, Pat?

PAT: Yes, I thought I'd pop round.

PETE: Well, find out all you can from her about Automat. The union Branch will probably respond better on Wednesday if they've got the facts in front of them.

PAT: Okay.

MARY: Yes, but we don't want to interfere, it's got to go through the proper channels.

PETE: All right. I only asked her to get the facts from her friend, not plant a bomb. (*He exits.*)

MARY: Pete will go too far one of these days.

PAT: What do you mean?

MARY: He doesn't know how the unions work.

PAT: He seems all right. It's okay to see Barbara tonight?

MARY: Tell her we'll do our best. Now let's get that fitter to check your machine.

(*They exit.*)

Scene 2

(*Enter PETE, with a large calculator.*)

PETE: Do you have a lot of trouble with your SMVs? How's your EFs? Do you wake up in the middle of the night worrying whether you've made a cock-up with the basic min? Here we are in the 1970s needing a pocket calculator to fight Work Study's assumptions about how we work, or how we should work, and yet down the road at Automat they're fighting to get the union recognised. Their boss Chamberlain must be a ruddy dinosaur. You'd think he'd realise it's 1976 and not 1876. It's been two months now since they first came out on strike and we've still failed to stop the firm. We've organised a rota for picketing the place. And a levy's been organised amongst the AUEW branches in Manchester. But some of the stories that have come out about the management there are unbelievable. Here at MEL's, management's getting all frustrated about this productivity deal. We tried to stop them bringing in Work Study – we said we wouldn't have it. But finally after telling us all their financial worries, most of the stewards agreed. With a million and a half people on the dole it's hard to fight what they said was necessary to ensure 'current levels of employment'. On my section you can sense the fear of unemployment. But they make out Work Study is a science, part of 20th-century industrial progress. Now if you want to get at a Work Study man, ask him how they work out effort rating. John's our secret weapon. If there ever was a bloke who could make out that you needed a fork-lift truck to pick up a cigarette, it's John. They've been watching him. I think we could probably spin this out for another 18 months with John being their guinea pig. Some of his scores are a 100 per cent effort for doing nothing. Even with this productivity deal it's a battle with management. And battle we will. I read the other day that Arnold Weinstock, chairman of GEC, MEL's is a subsidy of theirs, said that 'People are like elastic; the more work they have to do, the more they stretch.'

(*Enter* JOHN. PETE *and* JOHN *play cowboys having a duel with two large calculators.*)

JOHN: Okay, Pete, move over. This productivity deal isn't big enough for both of us.

PETE: You mean?

JOHN: Yep.

PETE: No!

JOHN: Yep, Standard Minimum Value ... FIVE UNITS!

(He fires by pressing down on calculator.)

PETE: Take Basic Minimum two. *(He fires and ducks.)*

JOHN: Times 4 per cent effort rating. *(He fires again. PETE falls across spanner as if shot dead by the last calculator round.)* Pete was a good shop steward but I've dedicated myself to clean up this machine shop of troublemakers. No one messes with me, Productivity Dealing Willie.

(Game over, PETE confronts JOHN for real.)

PETE: You know we're going down to the mass picket at Automat's tomorrow?

JOHN: Are you?

PETE: I said we are.

JOHN: I'm not that happy about it.

PETE: Neither are the 52 who've been stuck outside the gates for the last two months. Come on.

JOHN: God, I think I've just pulled a back muscle ... ooh ...

(PETE drags JOHN off.)

Scene 3

(Notice board is now reversed to show a picture of a tree. On the picket line; enter PAT and MARY.)

PAT: This is it.

MARY: What time do the pickets arrive?

PAT: Barbara said they'd be here at 5.30. Apparently the management make the scabs to go in early to avoid them.

MARY: You mean we might not even see them?

PAT: Depends. Barbara wasn't sure. She's really changed since this strike, you know.

MARY: How?

PAT: I can't really put my finger on it.

MARY: Fed up with it dragging on?

PAT: No, it's not that. She's more outgoing, confident.

MARY: I'd have thought she'd be less confident with the strike continuing.

PAT: She has her ups and downs. Helps me a lot with the kids. I had a row with Tom about her yesterday. He said he didn't want me to get involved, told me not to come down here today.

MARY: You don't have to stay, Pete and the others will be here soon. We won't miss you.

PAT: That's the last thing I want, Barbara's my friend. Besides, I agree with Pete. If the union doesn't win here, it's a defeat for all of us. I bet MEL's management is loving every minute of it.

MARY: But you don't want to make things worse for yourself.

PAT: They couldn't get any worse at home. I've decided that if Tom doesn't start to recognise who I am, what I might want, then he doesn't need me. What he needs is a skivvy, not me.

MARY: No sense in expecting too much. You've got a nice house, two lovely kids and . . .

PAT: Why can't I expect everything? I love my kids and a part of me still loves Tom. If we carry on like we are at the moment I might as well give it all up. I'm fed up of being told what to do, what to wear, what to think, how to bring the kids up, fed up with him, that foreman Carter, the lot of them.

MARY: In my day you'd be happy to have a husband who brought in a steady wage.

PAT: That was in those days, Mary, a long time ago. I want more than clearing up the shit after him and the kids. I want a life too. And thank God it's me there at my machine, and not Tom's wife.

(Enter PETE with radio.)

PETE: Stand aside girls, this picket is for Bionic Man. (Holds radio to chest.) Let me at the scabs. (In slow motion twiddles with knob, acts out kicking and throwing scabs in the air. Produces football made up like dummy with Chamberlain's face on it.) Take that, Chamberlain! (Hits ball to PAT, who strangles it.)

PETE: Careful with that managing director, we've got to go through the procedure. (Winks at MARY, PAT throws it back.)

PAT: He doesn't recognise the procedure.

PETE: That's all right, then. (Throws it over backdrop. A cry is heard – puzzled looks are exchanged.)

MARY: Where's John?

PETE: As soon as I told him about the mass picket, his old football injury struck him down. He's gone to the doctor's.

PAT: He makes my blood boil.

PETE: What do you expect from a Cockney Manchester United fan. Where's the aggro?

MARY: It's quiet at the moment.

PETE (looking around): So this is the factory that we've failed to bring to its knees. It doesn't look that scary. I imagined a little stone castle with a moat round it. I see it's got a Union Jack flying.

PAT: That's to warn the scabs there's a picket on! The management use it to signal to each other.

PETE: This would make a good film. *Chamberlain's Last Stand* or *I Buried my Head at Wounded Automat*.

(PETE moves over to tree. Meanwhile, MARY has been getting a station on the radio.)

MARY: Your voice was just on the radio.

PETE: Must be my new single. *(Pretends to sing.)*

MARY: It was. Stand by the tree again – say something.

PETE: 'This is stupid.'

PAT: There it is again.

PETE: I don't believe this. Do you think they've put a listening bug on this tree?

(From over the tree comes a big old-fashioned microphone.)

PETE: Look at this – they had this inconspicuous microphone hidden in the tree. *(PETE follows wire.)*

PAT: Well, that's got to take the cake.

PETE: The wire goes into that house there.

PAT: That's Automat's offices.

PETE *(down mike, in foreign accent)*: 'Ello, General Scanlon, Commander of Tank Division here. You vish to personally supervise the destruction of Automat? *(He pulls out wire.)* I wish that was true – it should give them something to worry about.

MARY: Careful Pete, that's going a bit far.

PETE: Words fail me with you sometimes, Mary.

(In bounces snap-happy REPORTER.)

REPORTER: Hello there ... comrades. *(Nudges PAT.)* News of

the World here full stop. Thought do feature on 'Factory of Hate' comma. Your side of the story for a change hey full stop.

MARY: We're all from MEL's Engineering down the road. And as fellow AUEW members we . . .

REPORTER: Kind of flying . . . *(Flaps arms.)* . . . picket *(Touches nose.)* . . . are you? *(Gets out pencil and paper.)*

PETE: If you want some material for a story there's plenty here.

PAT: Tell him about the microphone.

PETE: The Managing Director of this outfit thinks that by placing a microphone near the picket line he can find out what's going on, instead of talking to union reps. That flag is his signal to fellow scabs.

PAT: And the other day he sent one of them on to the road to throw a bucket of water down onto the pickets.

REPORTER: Yes, but what my readers want are the facts, something they can get their teeth into. I want something that hits 'em between the lines . . . eyes.

MARY: 'Factory of Hate'?

REPORTER: Comma. Exactly. The personal stories behind the headlines. Well observed . . . well observed . . . I tell you what. A picture speaks louder than words . . . Instant truth you might say. Can you line up? Look aggressive, that's it. Now, fearless grin, that's it . . . Lovely. And I wonder if you wouldn't mind . . . *(He gives MARY camera.)* . . . just taking a personal one for me . . . *(Comes over to PETE, puts him in pose with leg out, arm raised in air.)* Ready? Right now, big smile. *(PETE smiles in pose; REPORTER stands next to him.)* It's ready focused. After three then, one . . . two . . . *(He crouches in position next to PETE, to make out as if he's being punched and kicked.)* . . . three! Lovely, see you again. I'll send you a copy. That makes one to Special Branch, one to Trumid, one to . . . *(Snatches camera and exits.)*

PETE: What the . . .?

MARY: I thought he wanted our side of the story.

PAT: We should have been more careful.

PETE: If I see him again on this picket, I'll put that camera down his throat. *(Pause.)* I wish something would happen . . .

MARY: Things are happening. Blacking has started and we're putting pressure on to get third-party blacking.

PAT: Barbara's been on to a number of factories. Support is there.

MARY: It takes time for the blacking to take effect. You can't expect miracles overnight.

PETE: But it's not as if it's the first time – remember Roberts Arundel.

MARY: But they were broken.

PETE: After 18 months.

PAT: Why can't you two stop arguing? I don't see the reason for you constantly having a go at each other.

MARY: I've twenty years' experience in the union and when Pete starts on like some boy scout about do this, do that, you'd think he'd have the sense to listen to reason.

PETE: What bloody reason? You're still working for the same boss. He's still making money, probably more out of you now than 20 years ago. What's changed? Tell me.

MARY: When I first joined the union you had to battle. The unions in this country have changed it for the better. We fought so you could have a chance of a better education. I never had that.

PAT: I left school at 15, it was driving me mad.

MARY: But you had a chance.

PETE: There's God knows how many thousands of teachers on

the dole, and school leavers without jobs. I'm not saying you didn't fight for me and Pat, but you never controlled the country then, and we certainly don't control it now.

MARY: And we never will. Are you going to start telling me about socialism? I worked for it for twenty years and it's not come. And with the Labour government in power, it's as near as we'll ever get.

PAT: What's all this got to do with us?

PETE: Everything and nothing.

MARY: You're still wet behind the ears, Pete; you'll grow up and learn the facts of life. Once you settle down and have a family you'll know what life's all about.

PAT: Like my Tom, Mary?

MARY: I was an idealist once. Two husbands and twenty years working at MEL's made me see more clearly, and I know this much: the quicker you learn to accept how people are, the easier it will be for you. You can change things, but it takes time. It's different for you, Pat, I've been a woman in a man's world for a long time.

PETE: That's got nothing to do with it.

MARY: It's got a lot to do with it.

PETE: I mean I'm not an idealist, I've got only one life too. I'm not living in a dream world, I'm here on this picket line because I hate that boss inside that factory, just as much as I hate Bailey and his mob at MEL's. And if we can beat Chamberlain, then it helps me to know how to beat Bailey.

PAT: Why do you hate Bailey?

MARY: Because his kind always does hate.

PETE: God, is the way this country is at the moment what you spent twenty years fighting for? One and a half million on the dole, trade union leaders who say we've got to make the sacrifices and old age pensioners dying in freezing homes, eating cardboard.

PAT: Stop it, Pete.

PETE: But that's how things are. That's what you want me to see more clearly, Mary, I see it. What I want to know is how to fight it.

(*MARY walks off.*)

PAT: Why did you have to upset her like that? What have you got to be so smug about?

PETE: I wasn't being smug. It's just that talking with Mary sometimes it's hard to convince her that what she fought for hasn't yet been won. And for her own life, she kids herself it has been. I didn't want to upset her.

PAT: I'll tell you something. When I first came to this factory I didn't give a damn about the union. Oh, but I heard you, all the way from Section One, going on about it. But it was Mary that came to get me to join. Mary convinced me that I should join. If it had been left to you, and John, and —

PETE: John's not —

PAT: Let me finish. If it had been left to you and the other stewards, I wouldn't have had anything to do with your precious union. I didn't see much difference between you lot and my Tom, men telling me what to do, but Mary was different. She's worked hard to improve conditions here, and not just for women either. I've got a lot of respect for her, she's got a lot of guts and that's what I admire her for.

(*PAT attempts to go; PETE holds her back.*)

PETE: But do you know what I am going on about?

PAT: Sometimes I think I do.

(*They exit.*)

Scene 4

(Enter JOHN with red scarf.)

JOHN *(singing)*: Lou Macari. Lou Macari. *(To audience.)* You should have seen him, past the defence and then lined himself up for the shot. And it just went wide. Ah well, there's so much class at Manchester United, and if I could ever meet a girl who could thrill me in the penalty area like Pearson, I'd marry her tomorrow. Morning Mr Bailey, have you ever been thrilled in the penalty area? Suppose not. Monday morning, it's always the same. I wake up at 6.30 and fear grips me. I can't move, paralysed. But just for a second I imagine it's Friday morning. It's that thought that gets me up. But as soon as I get to the bus stop, the queue reminds me by the look on their faces. Monday's in the air and we could be professional mourners at a wake. My grandfather had a great wake. He came from Kerry. After ten hours non-stop drinking, he looked more alive than most of us lying around the coffin. My uncle Willie staggered to his feet, gave a toast: 'He was a whore of a man' and that started another bout.

(PETE creeps in.)

PETE *(in foreman's voice)*: Aren't you at your machine, Mr Fitzpatrick?

JOHN: I'm there. *(Jumps up in surprise until he sees who it is.)* You frightened the life out of me. Much more of that and MEL Engineering will lose the greatest centre half it's ever known, not to mention my union subs.

PETE: I didn't see you at the Automat picket on Thursday.

JOHN: I was coming, then my back started playing up. Went to the doctor's, it took hours. Place was filled with Pakis . . . *(PETE grabs JOHN by the throat.)* . . . people. He told me to take a day's rest, it's a bit better now. What happened, then? How did it go, then?

PETE: The picket was quite good, but we didn't see any scabs.

JOHN: So you extremists had a quiet day did you? (*PETE moves closer to him.*) I'm only joking. Did you see the *Evening News*? (*He hands PETE the paper.*) Sir Winston Churchill MP, grandson of the saviour of war-time Britain and friend of the working man, speaks.

PETE: The rubbish he writes. One of Jack's mates was telling me that Churchill's being asked to spread rumours about the pickets at Automat by Trumid.

JOHN: Tru who?

PETE: Trumid – it's the right wingers in the union, set up and backed by managements to split up the shop floor. Claims to be speaking for democracy.

(*Enter PAT and MARY laughing; MARY carrying notices for board.*)

(*PETE and JOHN read out from* Evening News.)

PETE: '61 pounds a week'? He must be joking . . . 'Only 10 per cent voted for the levy, not representative.' Usual crap.

MARY: Coming out with your friends now, are you John?

JOHN: What? (*Sees a Trumid flyer on notice board.*) Hey, who put that over United?

MARY (*to PETE*): Funny company you're keeping.

PAT: Will somebody tell me what's going on?

MARY: It seems our Joker John isn't just a funny man.

JOHN: I don't know what you're talking about.

PETE: Hang on a minute. John wouldn't put this over a picture of United.

PAT: Put what over what?

MARY: Who put it up if he didn't?

JOHN: I'd never even heard of Trumid until Pete just told me it was companies putting money behind right wingers.

MARY: That's what you are, aren't you?

JOHN: No.

MARY: You call yourself a moderate.

JOHN: Yes, but . . .

MARY: Well then.

JOHN (*going over to board and tearing down Trumid flyer*): It's not me.

PAT: It's hard to believe John could organise anything, let alone be whatever you think he is.

PETE: Pat's right.

MARY: I suppose so. But who else could it be?

PETE: We'd better tell the other stewards to watch out. It could always be one of the management.

PAT: Before you two dig trenches, could you tell me the enemy we're supposed to be so frightened of?

PETE: You tell her, Mary.

PAT: Thanks, Peter.

(*PETE is going towards JOHN; when he hears 'Peter' he turns, smiles, and walks back.*)

PETE: Sorry, Pat. (*To MARY.*) Read this: a friend of yours has written a letter to it.

(*PETE hands her the paper; JOHN takes poster of United and walks forward.*)

JOHN: Mary, you've got to believe me, it wasn't me. And if I catch the sod who stuck a Union Jack over Gerry Daly, I'll kill him. I admit that I don't know much about politics and the union but I'd never do this, not to Macari as well.

MARY: What are you talking about now?

JOHN: I'm saying I've got nothing to do with that midriff lot.

MARY: Okay.

JOHN: Oh.

MARY *(to PETE and PAT)*: He sounds just like his grandfather. *(PETE and PAT take note, JOHN shrugs.)* Churchill Junior! *(JOHN goes back to notice board.)* He must have had a good apprenticeship in his family's anti-union views.

PETE: Apprenticeship in dining with the Employers' Federation, more like.

MARY: 'We'll fight them on the beaches' – and in the mines. He set the troops on the miners.

PAT: At school they always said he was a hero. We watched his funeral on the school telly. One of the teachers was crying.

MARY: My tears were for those who died, not for the warmonger he was. Most of them who died fought against fascism, for freedom. Some said Hitler admired Churchill.

JOHN: HORACE!

PETE: Who?

JOHN: Horace, the early morning cleaner. He's in here first thing, he'd have the opportunity.

PAT: Talk to him Pete, otherwise Columbo won't let us out of work tonight until he gets a suspect.

PETE: It wouldn't be Horace.

JOHN: Why not? He looks suspicious.

PETE: They might be undercover, this Trumid lot, but they're more likely to be driving directors' cars. It's not Horace.

JOHN: I thought you said they were infiltrating the union.

PETE: They are, but they're not starting with Horace and working their way up. They've already got friends in high places, our tuba-playing Salvation Army General Secretary for one.

(*JOHN makes the sign of the cross.*)

PETE: What's that for?

JOHN: Shrewd move, using a Proddy.

PETE: What's that got to do with it?

JOHN: No one would spot him. I remember my father telling us about Bill Carron. Now *he* was a real leader, and a good Catholic.

MARY: And the most right-wing leader we ever had. It took us 13 years to get rid of him and his Carron's Laws.

PETE: Sir William Carron, the only head of a British trade union to retire with 19 company directorships, against union rules.

MARY: I remember. He went to the TUC Congress and voted for a wage freeze, when union workers voted against it.

JOHN: But even the Pope honoured him.

PETE: That sounds like Carron. Between the Employers' Federation and the Pope, he never had much time for rank and file members of the union.

JOHN: God rest his soul.

PAT: Well, is Columbo about to make an arrest? If so, I'll go and get some work done. (*She exits.*)

JOHN (*in Columbo accent*): Okay, Miss, but don't leave town – I might want to question you later.

MARY: It's funny that this Trumid business has come up just at the time that we've gone to picket Automat's.

PETE: Just after we've foiled Work Study for another six months as well.

MARY: Coincidence?

PETE: Well, I don't want to be too paranoid, but management's been very quiet these last few weeks.

MARY: That's just the holidays.

PETE: I hope so. Let's not make too much of it at the moment. But I'd love to know who this Trumid bloke is.

(Meanwhile, JOHN has been doing Columbo actions in the background.)

PETE: Any advances on Horace, John?

JOHN *(still in Columbo voice)*: Sorry? *(Snaps out of it.)* Sorry?

MARY *(to PETE)*: I'll be your alibi if he tries to arrest you. *(Exits.)*

PETE *(American accent)*: Who's the Trumid man?

JOHN: Well, I've whittled it down to a tuba-playing Catholic driving a director's car who's a . . . *(He holds up United picture.)* . . . City supporter. *(Exit PETE.)* *(To audience.)* I'm getting more confused than ever. We are a democratic union, with a postal ballot – you can't get any more democratic than that. Mind you, the last ballot paper that came through my letterbox got eaten by the dog. But surely it can't be as bad as Pete and Mary say it is? I mean, how do these leaders get elected anyway? It's just that the moderates are winning the elections. What have I got to worry about? I'm moderate. But it makes you wonder with this Trumid lot. If they're backed by management they can't be on our side, can they? I've worked in industry long enough to know that when it comes down to it, management look after their own, and the unions look after theirs. It's two sides of the coin, the same coin. Just two sides. But who are the moderates, then? *(Takes out coin from pocket.)* I suppose we're the crinkly bits round the edge. *(Exits.)*

Scene 5

(Enter PAT.*)*

PAT *(to audience)*: It happened this morning. Tom and me actually spoke to each other for the first time in what seems like months. He was on a late, but he was awake when I got up. He *asked* me what I was doing tonight. I've been going round to Barbara's after work as she's been minding Gary for me. It's given Mum a break too. And he asked me what I was doing, instead of his hinting about what I should do. He even showed interest when I told him what was happening down at Automat's. I suppose I'm being silly really, but it felt as though a weight's been taken off me. All he did was ask.

(Enter JOHN, *reading crumpled letter.)*

JOHN: Hi ya.

PAT: Good morning, John. *(*JOHN *is taken aback by* PAT's *friendliness.)* Did you catch the person who defaced United?

JOHN: Yes.

PAT: Who was it?

JOHN: Eh? Oh no, I don't know who did it.

PAT: What's the matter with the joker this morning?

JOHN: Nothing. Well, I think it's nothing. Horace dug this out of Bailey's waste paper basket. *(He hands it to* PAT.*)* He told me to give it to Pete.

PAT: It's just a memo to Bailey.

JOHN: Horace seemed to think it was important. He's a strange old bloke. He sifts through all the rubbish in the offices. He says you can tell a lot about a person from their rubbish. One day he came across an invitation for Bailey to attend the Annual Police Dance. He phoned through a bomb warning. It was in all the papers – they had to call it off. He hates the police, ever since they sent him down for three months for indecently exposing himself to a traffic warden.

PAT: Traffic warden?

JOHN: Strange old bloke, Horace.

PAT (*reads*): 'Mr Leaman requests submission of report re. present industrial relations for November 14 meeting of Board. VITAL FOR ENACTMENT OF PROPOSED RECOMMENDATIONS.' What's it mean?

JOHN: I've no idea. Probably Horace needs to meet an aging traffic warden and find true love. If I got you the uniform could you . . .

(*They both laugh. Enter* MARY *and* PETE.)

PETE: Until the guard gets refitted, Mike doesn't work on it.

MARY: They said it'll be two weeks before they can get a replacement.

PETE: And Mike's only got two arms to lose. Let them solve it, it's their problem.

JOHN (*in Russian voice*): New instructions have just come on ze teleprinter from Moscow, comrade. (*Hands* PETE *memo.*) Horace gave it to me for you.

PETE: Horace?

PAT: The cleaning demon flasher.

JOHN: He picked it up in Bailey's office. Said you'd understand it. We can't work out what it means.

PETE (*to* MARY): Read that.

MARY: Oh no.

PAT: Don't keep us in suspense.

PETE: Well, if it's what I think it is, management are gearing up for a fight.

PAT: What over?

PETE: You know they said that the productivity deal was a necessity to ensure present levels of employment?

PAT: Yes.

PETE: Well, they didn't get their deal, did they?

PAT: Do you think they want to force it on us?

PETE: No, you see Leaman is a member of the GEC board, and Chairman of MEL's. He wouldn't be involved in pushing for a departmental matter like productivity.

MARY: What Pete's trying to say is that he thinks that management are about to propose redundancies.

JOHN: But I remember a while back you said that management if anything were hoping to expand production. There was no mention of redundancies.

PETE: They mean mechanise.

PAT: But we're not sure yet, it could mean anything. Why are you reading so much into a bit of paper?

PETE: It's just a feeling.

PAT: Well, what are we going to do?

MARY: We'll have to meet management to find out for sure. All the paper does is warn us. At least we can be on our toes.

PETE: I knew something was in the air. Those bastards!

PAT: You sound as if you're already outside the gates. If they're brewing for a fight they can have one.

MARY: It's not as easy as that, love.

PETE: Pat's right, let's prepare for the worst.

JOHN: I don't know what you're so worried about, Pete, they'll never finish us, we're skilled. Besides, we're the backbone of MEL's First Eleven.

PAT: Trust you, John, you don't give a damn about anyone but yourself, do you?

JOHN: I'm just seeing sense. I am sorry if anyone has to go down the road, but . . .

PETE: Just hold on, will you? No one's going down the road if we can help it.

MARY: For heaven's sake, let's meet management and talk about it. We're just working ourselves up for nothing.

PETE: We'd better hold a stewards' meeting first. I'll do some checking up and see if I can find out anything more about their plans.

JOHN: Look. If it's just because we've been messing them about over the productivity deal, let's come clean and let them go through with it.

PETE: It's not that. MEL's is just one firm under the wing of GEC. They plan on an international scale, and part of their plan is rationalisation. You can bet that if they're planning redundancies, the decision will be made at a GEC board meeting, and will probably mean redundancies not just at MEL's but at the other factories. The productivity deal was just to test our shop-floor strength.

MARY: I don't see how all this is going to help. We work at MEL's, we know the management here and we can negotiate with them over redundancies. Oh, you're getting me at it now.

PAT: I can't afford to lose my job here. Why did this have to happen now?

JOHN: You could always get a sweet shop with your redundancy money.

PETE: It's not funny, John, okay? *(Exits.)*

JOHN: I was only saying. *(Follows* PETE *off.)*

PAT: I feel sick. I was on top of the world earlier too. I think you're right, Mary, I should settle for what I've got.

MARY: No, you were right before. Never settle for what you've got. I never did. Just never expect to get what you want. Fight for it, struggle for it, just don't expect to get it. Somehow fighting for what you want changes what you thought you wanted in the first place.

*(*PAT *kisses her and exits.)*

MARY *(to audience)*: I am tired. Pete's so sure of himself. Redundancy! I've been facing it all my life. I'm not sure I can fight it off this time. It's got to be fought, but I don't know if I want to. I'm 51 in January. Nine years off state-enforced redundancy. Whether I want it or not they'll tell me my work's finished. I can die then, can I? I was 18 when I started work in the ammunitions factory near Bath. I worked, ate and slept 400 feet underground. I never saw the sky except at weekends. The bombing was bad in Bath and Bristol and you could feel the earth shake. The caverns were huge. When I first saw them I didn't believe it – about two thousand of us worked down there. They were some great times. Most of all though, the solidarity. All of us together. That's where I got my education. I joined the union and we had to fight even there. Some of the girls said the union was stopping us helping the country to survive the Germans. They never seemed to see that no matter what the war was about, Vickers and BAC and the others were making fortunes from it. I used to have this nightmare that they'd keep us down those caverns forever, wouldn't bother telling us the war was over, just keep us working. When I did get out at the end of the war, I came back to Vickers in Trafford Park. I realised that they needed us above ground. Well, we had to have a house, to fill it with the fruits of the victories of war – television, motorcars, new furniture . . . and now? I don't know. Pete does though. I fought for the wages that bought those things. I negotiated the best rates for the job. And for most of them here, that's all they want. Well, I fought so they could have them. Let them fight to keep them if that's what they want. But me? I just don't know.

(She exits.)

Scene 6

(Enter PAT with JOHN following on her heels. She pins a 'Social for Automat' flyer on the notice board.)

JOHN: I was wondering what was happening at Automat.

PAT: There's a social on Friday, called by the District. Are you coming?

JOHN: Now you're talking. I'll be there.

PAT: It's only a social evening, you know, nothing to get excited about.

JOHN: Well, I want to support them as best I can.

PAT: Downing pints is your idea of solidarity, is it?

JOHN: Now look, let's get something straight, I'm twisted.

PAT: I hope your insanity isn't contagious.

JOHN: It's a very selective madness. I don't think you'll catch it, I got it from management.

PAT: You could do a turn at the social on Friday. Tell a few jokes?

JOHN: I could do my impression of a magician.

PAT: That sounds good.

JOHN: You see, I take five pounds from the audience at random. Then you watch me disappear.

PETE (*entering*): Pat, have you seen Mary?

PAT: Not this morning.

JOHN: Revolution's started without her, has it?

PETE: Management called a meeting for Friday morning. I've heard they are going to call for redundancies.

PAT: I forgot all about that.

PETE: I don't know how many though, and we don't know when they're going to press for them.

JOHN: There's nothing we can do at the moment anyway. I was speaking to Jack in Section Five. If they propose voluntary redundancies, he says he knows four blokes that would leave.

PETE: That's not the point. It doesn't matter how many want to go. It's what we're left with. Over the last five years this firm has 'lost' 250 jobs. 480 of us work at MEL's and we produce double the amount of goods now than we did then.

JOHN: That's because of their investment in new machinery.

PETE: I'll grant you we have had some new equipment. But that production has increased by the ludicrous amount of overtime some of the blokes have to do in order to get a decent wage.

PAT: What can we do?

PETE: Well, I've spoken with the stewards and they think we should resist all attempts to make more redundancies, and the first thing to go will be the overtime.

JOHN: You'll have your work cut out to convince some of the blokes of that.

PETE: You're not kidding. I've already had a big bust-up with Ted. What with the fear of the dole, labour-saving machinery, productivity deals and overtime, it's just getting to me what a mess we're in.

JOHN: You made your bed, now lie in it.

PETE: It's all my fault. Thank you, John.

JOHN: Well, you've got to consider the country in all this.

PETE: We are the bloody country. Who do you mean? The shareholders of GEC?

JOHN: I'm just saying that everyone says we're in a crisis. We know we've all got to tighten our belts.

PETE: If I hear any more bullshit from you, I'll ram it down your throat.

JOHN: It's a fact though, isn't it?

PETE: The government and the TUC say businesses must invest to cut unemployment. But when they do, they buy the latest labour-saving machinery. That's a fact too. We're being conned. We've always been conned.

PAT: What happens now, then?

PETE: I wish I had all the answers, but we can start on these present plans for redundancies.

PAT: I'm with you – don't look so harassed.

PETE: Ta. I wish I knew where Mary is. Tell her I'm with Jack, if you see her.

(He exits.)

JOHN: Deep thinker, our Pete.

PAT: At least he talks straight. What's your view on it?

JOHN: Well, I go along with Pete up to a point. But I always remember what an old bloke who I served my time with used to say, 'Take the money and say nothing.'

PAT: That's really going to help us, that is.

JOHN (*singing*): 'If I can help somebody some of the time, then my living has not been in vain . . .'

(*They exit.*)

(*Enter* PETE *and* MARY.)

MARY: We still don't know for sure. Let's see what they say.

PETE: For Christ's sake, we've got to be responsible for giving a lead in this. We can't just lay our heads on the chopping block, and ask Bailey to hang on for a minute while we get organised.

MARY: What do you suggest, then?

PETE: On the basis of rumour alone, cut out the overtime. With 18,000 engineers in the District on the dole, we should have done it anyway.

MARY: Well, all right.

PETE: I was expecting you to argue over that one.

MARY: No, you might be right. I've nothing against an overtime ban.

PETE: We'll get together before Friday, then?

MARY: Thursday dinner.

(*She starts to go.* PAT *comes in;* MARY *walks out, straight past.*)

PAT: Mary?

PETE: Perhaps she's feeling down about the redundancies.

PAT: I've never seen her look like that before about anything.

PETE: I wish I knew what's going on with her. If she's going to crack up, she can wait until after this. She's got to be on her toes for it.

PAT: If you'd stop rowing with her, perhaps she'd have a chance. It's probably you bringing her down.

PETE: What have I got to do with it?

PAT: Every time you two are alone you're going off at each other about something.

PETE: It's not just for the sake of arguing. We have to work things out between us.

(Enter JOHN.)

JOHN: Watch out. I've just seen the phantom of the MEL morgue. Mary, silently passing Inspection like a ghost. She didn't even curse me as she went.

PAT: Were you having a smoke by the Stores?

PETE: I thought this afternoon was your doctor's appointment?

JOHN (to PAT): No. (To PETE.) Yes. Interrogation over?

PETE: What are you doing here, then?

JOHN: If you'd let me get a word in, I'll tell you. (Hands box marked 'AUTOMAT' to PETE.)

PETE and PAT: Where did you get that?

JOHN: I just happened to be passing Stores and Albert gave it me. Said that there was a boxful delivered unmarked two weeks ago, and he found this one with a label on this morning.

PAT: But when the trouble started at Automat you said that we never had anything from them.

PETE: No, we didn't have anything to black, then.

JOHN: What's this, Christmas cake?

PETE: The crafty sods. This is the way management think they can support our dear friend Chamberlain.

PAT: They've started ordering from Automat's to give the scabs work.

PETE: No wonder they can advertise at above District rates for scab labour. They've probably more orders now than they've ever had.

PAT: Barbara said the blacking was going quite well.

PETE: I'm sure it is, where the stuff is recognised. But you can't black goods if you don't know where they come from. *(He peels off the Automat label.)* We'll check through the Stores order books, see if there's any more to be delivered. *(Wipes forehead.)* As if we didn't have enough on our plate.

JOHN: We've got too much on it, if you ask me.

PAT: What, moaner?

JOHN: We've got problems of our own, here. We can't afford the time running around fighting other people's battles for them.

PETE: That's great, coming from you. What did you ever do to support Automat? Come to think of it, what have you ever done to support anything the union's pushed for, except your wages?

JOHN: I support you and Mary to do it for me.

PETE: Right. For a start, you can start pulling your own weight. You check Albert and the Stores. See Jack if you need any help at tracing where those transformers went. No, on second thoughts, you'd be better checking up, Pat. It needs guts to tackle Albert.

JOHN: I've got guts.

PAT: The hard man speaks.

PETE: So now you're supporting the Automat strike. Aren't you worried about your reputation as a moderate?

PAT: I can see the headlines in the works paper. 'Leading factory moderate transformered'. *(Points to box.)*

JOHN: I am being intimidated ... threatened – and I'll let you know what I find out about these later. *(Exits.)*

PAT: He's almost human sometimes.

PETE: Only from the neck down. Most of his brains are in his feet. Automat – it's been months now. The Confederation are handling it as well. All that time. Place should have been sorted ages ago. I feel I'm hitting my head against a brick wall.

PAT: You're doing well, everyone's behind you.

PETE: I don't need anyone behind me. I want us all there.
480 heads hitting the wall might knock the bloody thing down.

PAT: Or give us all sore heads.

PETE: We can't stop redundancies with me going into management telling them where to get off. If I'm on my own they'll put me top of the list.

PAT: We wouldn't let that happen, we'd be out the gate.

PETE: I know, but we'll have to stick together. But what I'm frightened of is if we don't, we'll end up accepting voluntary redundancies, while management back track on the productivity deal. So we'll come out thinking it's a victory and then they'll wait three months, maybe six months, until the next time. And the bloody farce will start all over again.

PAT: But you're underestimating us. We're right behind you and Mary.

PETE: Mary?

PAT: Why do you say it like that?

PETE: It's Mary I'm worried about. I can't put my finger on it. She's quiet.

PAT: We've just been through that.

PETE: It's not just me and her having a row. I'll see what happens at Thursday dinner.

PAT: I don't see what you're making all the fuss about.

PETE: Mary was the best negotiator we ever had. Being a woman didn't hinder her, she always fought like hell. But she never thought the backing from the shop floor was important, it was her upping the rates, we had one of the best basic rates in Manchester. And Mary got it, with the support of the other stewards and the 'ayes' at the mass meeting. But she never bothered involving anyone except the stewards, it was her that put me forward, no one else wanted to do it anyway. Mary taught me the procedure, I learnt a lot from watching her. Not copying her. Because she made mistakes, I learnt from them too. And I get the feeling that now Mary might not see what's really at stake.

(Enter JOHN carrying large box.)

JOHN *(throws box to them)*: Here you are: mission accomplished. Twenty-four transformers – 'Return to Sender'. Careful though, I accidentally smashed three bottles of tricoethylene over them as I repacked them. Upset me, that did.

PAT: Three? You were fast.

JOHN: Well, now you know why the whole country fears Stretford Enders. We're taking over. Today MEL's, tomorrow the world.

PETE: Not with Tommy Docherty, you won't.

JOHN: You don't have to rub it in. I remember him at Chelsea. *(Out to audience.)* We really will have to get rid of him, you know. *(To PETE.)* Wait a minute, you smiled! Did you see that, he actually smiled! I'll make a note of that – it should get on the front page of the Salford *City Reporter*. By the way, Albert said there's two more deliveries of these parcels in two weeks' time. So if you want – I mean, we want – to start blacking, we'd better put it to a mass meeting. Over and out, Roger.

PAT: Quite the union organiser now.

JOHN: Well, of course my special qualities help along that line – seeking fame and cushy jobs, making words roll off my tongue. *(In Northern accent.)* 'Brothers and sisters . . .' *(PETE chucks box back.)* Are you coming to the home game tonight?

(They exit.)

Scene 7

(Enter PAT, and MARY with notice: 'AUEW and T&G Mass Meeting, Monday 12.00' Rips down another Trumid notice on board.)

PAT: Pete says he'll see you in the canteen, Mary.

(MARY continues to fiddle with board.)

MARY: Tell him I'll be there.

PAT: You'll see him before me, won't you?

MARY: I've got a lot of work on this morning, I'm not sure I'll be able to make it before dinner.

PAT: What's going on between you two?

(MARY shakes head and shrugs shoulders.)

PAT: Snap out of it. Come on.

(MARY just looks tiredly at PAT.)

PAT: I'm only trying to help.

MARY: I know. It's not just Pete. Thanks for your cheery words though.

PAT: They're not meant to be 'cheery'. I said let me help.

MARY: How's Tom and the kids?

PAT: Fine. *(Looks straight at MARY.)* I said can I help, and you're asking how I am!

(Enter JOHN.)

JOHN *(chanting)*: 'You're gonna get your fuc—' ... *(Notices the women and stops chant.)* Big day tomorrow then, Mary? Trenches dug? Don't worry, I've decided to come and meet management with you, I'll be there. No nonsense this time. A quick warm up round the Fabrication Shop, then we'll be off, into the game. I'll pass to Pete, we'll play a 4-4-2 formation for the first ten minutes, then you raid them on the wing, play havoc with their defence, then the long ball from that dozy T&G steward Bert, up to me. I'll round Bailey, slip the ball through that production manager's legs, Pete worries that toff Leaman in the penalty area, then you take up the far post, I cross and a fabulous diving header from you – it's a goal! United! United! No danger. Should be at least 12–0 by half time.

MARY: It's not a game.

JOHN: I'm only having a laugh.

MARY: Well go and play somewhere else.

JOHN: I know, this place is like a morgue . . .

PAT: Shouldn't you be working?

JOHN: That's the last time I'll try and bring some sunshine into your lives.

PAT: Shine somewhere else.

(JOHN *shrugs and remains on stage, with his back to the women.*)

(*Enter* PETE.)

PETE: I can't make it at dinner after all. I'll have to have a word with you now.

MARY: I'm not sure if I've got the time.

PETE: Well, make time.

MARY: Look, it's quite straightforward from what happened at yesterday's stewards' meeting, you all seem sure that we'll ban overtime and refuse to accept any redundancies.

PETE: But you said bugger all last night.

MARY: It was all said for me.

PETE: Come off it, Mary.

MARY: We can't win, no matter what you say.

previous page: Ernest Dalton (John) rehearsing <u>Just a Cog</u>, Scene 1

(below, l to r) Penny Morris (Mary), Ernest, Newman Smith (Pete) and Elsie Hallsworth (Pat) in <u>Just a Cog</u> Scene 5 at Moderna Ltd, Mytholmroyd, West Yorkshire, in 1977. John: 'New instructions have just come on ze teleprinter from Moscow, comrade ...'

(above right) Holding the audience at Moderna

(below right) AUEW official (with Newman standing behind) after <u>Just a Cog</u> at Moderna. The noticeboard is one of the props

(above left) Audience at Moderna, about to get ...

(below left) Newman, Scene 8: 'I was born when "we never had it so good" ...'

(above) Elsie and company rehearsing <u>Just a Cog</u> Scene 3: 'I was an idealist once ...'

(left) Ernest (Ferry) in <u>Partisans</u>, Scene 4: '"Yeah,
Greedy here!" and I ate them too! ...'

(above, l to r) Penny (Hammer), Chris (Mole), Newman
(Birdman) and Ernest rehearsing Scene 1: 'If I'd
have known, I'd have got dressed up ...'

(above) Newman and Chris in Scene 5: 'He was the first one to call me Mole ...'

(below) Chris in Scene 1: 'a moat 4-foot wide ...'

(right) Penny in Scene 6: 'I'm not the only one. There's plenty more in the same boat ...'

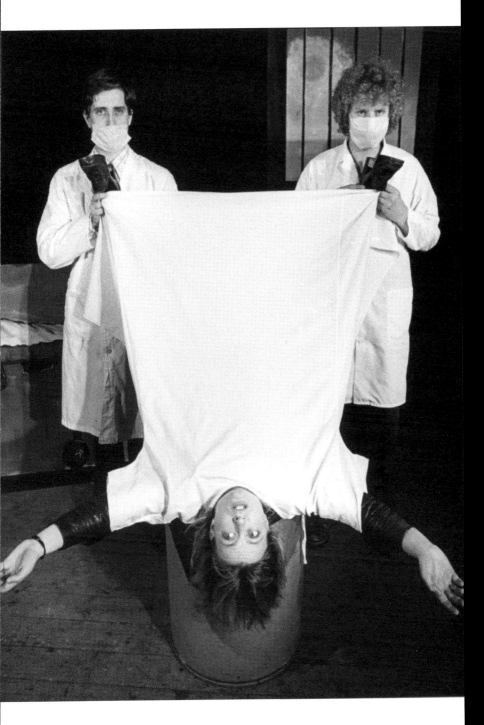

(above) <u>Safety First or Last?</u>: Elsie and Newman at British Leyland works canteen, Birmingham, October 1976

(above right) Penny and Ernest doing the Safety play at Pork Farms Canteen, Nottingham, September 1976.

(below right) Hanky trick warm-up (with participation)

(below) Audience for the Safety play at Manchester Dry
Docks in July 1975. Maureen Ramsay, Spanner administrator,
with her daughter, is on the far left

(right) Move over, Des O'Connor: Spanner makes front-page
news in <u>The Stage</u>. The controversy led Spanner to call the
Conference to Defend the Arts against Political Censorship,
in December 1977 in Salford

he Stage
and
ELEVISION TODAY

No 5041

November 24, 1977

robe into recent political arts 'vetting' raises

ying implications for devolution

TORY COUNCILLOR SHAKES UP LOCAL GRANTS

ROBIN THORNBER
reports from Lancashire

THE Arts Council's new policy of devolving responsibility to the regional arts associations has suffered its first setback — almost as soon as the process had begun to get under way.

The controversy caused by North West Arts' decision to investigate the "political views and aims" of one of its major clients, the North West Spanner theatre company, before renewing their grant has highlighted the problem of the regional arts associations' vulnerability to political pressure from local authority representatives.

North West Spanner evolved out of a community theatre group called Inroads, which worked mainly in children's street theatre in the tougher parts of York and then Salford.

For the past five years they have specialised in reaching non-theatre audiences, performing in factory canteens and working men's clubs with shows about safety at work, redundancies in the textile industry, and the conflict between militants and moderates in the trade unions.

Their grant for 1977/8 was £12,000 from the Arts Council of Great Britain and £7,000 from North West Arts. Last month North West Arts' drama panel recommended that Spanner should be "devolved" from next April, with a combined grant of £24,500 for 1978/9 being channelled through North West Arts.

But the association's management council decided on October 7 not to include any subsidy to North West Spanner in its estimates for the next year — until the group's "artistic standards and political views and aims" had been investigated.

A sub-committee consisting of four Conservative councillors, a former Liberal councillor, and the chairman of the drama panel (David Scase), was asked to report back on December 16. But Scase, artistic director of the Manchester Library Theatre Company, refused to join in the investigation.

"We have spent months assessing the artistic standards of this group," Scase said. "Their material is exactly geared to the audiences they are working for. We do not have a critical role as to what the content should be. This is not the thin end of the wedge, it is the wedge itself."

The investigation into North West Spanner's politics was proposed by Greater Manchester County Councillor John Kershaw, the Conservative prospective parliamentary candidate for Stalybridge and Hyde and a supporter of the National Association for Freedom.

"Grants ought not to be made to organisations whose primary aim is to put forward political propaganda," said Kershaw, "and it is my view that North West Spanner appear to be putting forward Marxist views."

Asked if he thought every theatre company should be vetted for opinions which might offend Conservative councillors, Kershaw replied: "I don't object to people presenting a wide range of political opinions, but I don't think there should be unbridled, unfettered freedom."

Kershaw did not accept that the introduction of political criteria into arts association assessments was unprecedented, although he agreed that "I may have raised something with wider implications". He would, he said, be scrutinising every grant application which came to North West Arts on the same basis.

The northern area committee of Equity later condemned the "witch hunt activities of the North West Arts management council" and called for a trade union inquiry into "the composition and administration of North West Arts".

North West Spanner is refusing to co-operate with the investigation. Penny Morris, one of its founder members, said: "We understand Councillor Kershaw has seen only part of one of our performances whereas the drama advisers at both the Art Council and North West Arts have seen many performances and have studied and assessed every aspect of our work over a number of years. We are confident of their support and that of our large grass roots audience in the north west and nationally."

The Arts Council's secretary-general, Roy Shaw, said that his officers had spoken well of the group's work. "The Arts Council makes no political judgements, only artistic ones, and it would deplore the introduction into the world of the arts of any form of political discrimination."

David Edgar, Henry Livings, and Adrian Mitchell are to speak at a conference North West Spanner is calling on the implications of political criteria into artistic assessments. It will be held on Sunday, December 4 at 4 and 2.30pm at the Peter Green Community Centre, Corporation Street, Salford 3. The organiser is Spanner's administrator, Maureen Ramsay (telephone 061 881 7845).

The Stage and TELEVISION TODAY

December 22, 1977   No 5045

SPARKS FLY OVER NORTH WEST SPANNER

Angry meeting rejects 'official' report

Manchester — North West Spanner, the Manchester-based touring company was rescued from the political chop by North West Arts Association last Friday (December 16), reports Robin Thornber.

The association's management council last month voted by 23-13 to set up a sub-committee to investigate Spanner's "artistic standards and political aims" after a Conservative councillor representing the Greater Manchester County, John Kershaw, had objected that the group appeared to be spreading Marxist views.

But last week's management council meeting, after voting to exclude the press, agreed by 36 votes to 22 merely to "receive and note" the report of the investigative subcommittee, which recommended refusal of Spanner's grant on the grounds that

1 the group had no constitution;
2 it had failed to provide financial information;
3 it used productions as a preliminary to political discussion;
4 it stages productions in private clubs (ie Labour clubs).

The sub-committee, which consisted of four Conservative councillors after the chairman of NWA's drama panel refused to join it and

the one Liberal dissented from the report, criticised the officers of the association for their lack of co-operation. "The information provided was tardy, slovenly, minimal, grudgingly given, and in some aspects biased," their report said.

But the management council, which was unusually well attended, then voted by acclaim in favour of a rival report by the association's drama panel, which reasserted its recommendation that a grant of £24,500 (including devolved funds from ACGB) to North West Spanner should be included in the estimates for 1978/9.

The drama panel's report also laid down as general principles:

1 that recommendations for grant aid should be made regardless of an organisation's political viewpoint;
2 that the content of art forms was adequately covered by existing legislation;
3 that the management council should refer back panel recommendations with which it was not satisfied.

The GMC councillors who supported the investigation objected after the meeting to the "implied threat" in a statement by the Arts

Council's deputy secretary-general, Angus Stirling.

Stirling had said that "there was no issue on which the Arts Council would take a graver view" than a resolution to withdraw subsidy on political grounds.

The GMC councillors said that they would have to think very hard about the GMC's £83,000 grant to North West Arts.

Penny Morris, a founder member of North West Spanner, said at a celebrity performance at the West End Community Centre in Ashton-under-Lyne: "I'm not sure that we want to be funded through North West Arts now, anyway."

(above left) 'The group appeared to be spreading Marxist views' shock horror probe ...

(below left) Some tickets for Spanner productions

(above right) David Edgar (playwright) and (below right) Roland Muldoon (Director of CAST) speaking at the Salford conference in December 1977

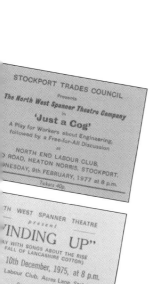

STOCKPORT TRADES COUNCIL
Presents
The North West Spanner Theatre Company
in
'Just a Cog'
A Play for Workers about Engineering,
followed by a Free-for-All Discussion
at
NORTH END LABOUR CLUB,
ROAD, HEATON NORRIS, STOCKPORT.
NESDAY, 9th FEBRUARY, 1977 at 8 p.m.
Tickets 40p

TH WEST SPANNER THEATRE
present
"INDING UP"
AY WITH SONGS ABOUT THE RISE
FALL OF LANCASHIRE COTTON)
10th December, 1975, at 8 p.m.
Labour Club, Acres Lane, Stalybridge

(standing, l to r) David Calder (actor), Henry Livings (playwright); (seated, l [patterned jumper] to r) Howard Brenton, David Hare and John McGrath (playwrights). At the Conference to Defend the Arts against Political Censorship, Salford, December 1977

PETE: We let them do what they like to do?

MARY: I just feel at the moment it might be best, if they propose voluntary redundancies, to accept.

PETE: How can you say that? Just stand by and watch men and women go down the road?

MARY: Management won't be asking for more than 50 redundancies and I bet there's that number would jump at the chance to take the money and be off.

PETE: And what of their jobs? Another 50 jobs in engineering? We should be fighting to make more jobs available, not less.

MARY: What are you going to do? Force the shop floor to stop overtime? You'll have a job. Most of them couldn't care about anything, only themselves. You're in for a shock if you think they'll ban overtime.

PETE: We wouldn't need to if we fought for a decent basic wage.

MARY: And the 35-hour week?

PETE: Yes, and why not?

MARY: I've had enough, Pete. It's over to you, with all your illusions. If you believe those things, then carry on, if you won't listen.

PETE: Listen to what? All you're telling me is it's impossible. Just like Bailey saying it's impossible, we must have redundancies. You've fought them all the way before. When I first came here, we didn't even have a decent bog to wash the crap off our hands – they said then new bogs was impossible.

MARY: You don't have to tell me whose side I'm on.

PETE: I wish I didn't. I don't know what's happened to you, Mary.

MARY: Perhaps the 15 years I've been working here make me able to see things a little bit better than you.

PETE: I'd have hoped they would, but all you're saying is don't fight, we can't fight.

MARY: I'm a lot older than you, a lot more experienced.

PETE: Look, you've negotiated all your life, it's harder now. We almost have to threaten to walk out the gates every time we want a cracked cup changed in the canteen. It's different, the battle's changed. We don't fight just the employer now, when we ask for more money – we have to take on the TUC, the government, the press, the bloody lot.

MARY: The Social Contract is here to stay, if that's what you're going on about. And the trade unions voted to accept it.

PETE: For the closing of schools, hospitals, for building no more council houses and watching the dole queues getting longer and longer!

MARY: No.

PETE: That's right, most people accepted the Social Contract to stop those things.

MARY: But you'll never change the way people are, and I'll bet there's a good few here who don't give a damn for your ideals.

PETE: Like you.

MARY: I never said that.

PETE: You are a lot older than me and I respect you. But I'll never see the world the way you do. Just like I'll never accept defeat the way you feel it. Because all I've ever known is wage freezes, Tory phases one to twenty, and now the Social Contract. In my life, I've not seen or gained anything – I've only watched the way we live getting worse. You tell me you've seen it get better. Well, I haven't. I want it better.

MARY: You're right, I *have* seen them get better. I worked and slogged my guts out to make sure everyone here got as much as I could get out of management and not just money. I was the one that ran round doing the boring chores, getting people their Supplementary Benefit, trying to get them to come to Branch meetings, to take an active part in the union. They'd prefer to do nothing. Apathetic. I did everything. Well, now I've decided I've stopped.

PETE: But that was the problem. You say in one breath the shop floor are apathetic and won't take an active part in the Branch and then turn round and say you did everything. Now not you, me, Jack or any of the stewards can afford to be on our own. We need an army, the days of the generals are over. We've got to fight these redundancies and we need everyone on the shop floor together. And I want to know what you're going to say on Monday.

MARY: I won't say anything. Is that what you wanted?

PAT: Mary! It could be me that has to go.

MARY: Pete's got a lifetime in front of him. He's young and got no ties. It's different for you with Tom and the kids.

PAT: That's all the more reason why we must stop them, surely? I want the best life for my kids – how can I give it to them not knowing if I'll be in work from one minute to the next?

MARY: You'll just have to make the best of it. Oh, I don't know . . . (She is upset and leaves.)

JOHN: Daft old bag.

PETE: She's worth ten of you, so shut up.

PAT: What will she do?

PETE: I don't know. I'm not even sure she knows.

JOHN: Well, we'd better get some work done today otherwise we won't have a factory to worry about. It's funny, but my stars said there might be tensions at work. Amazingly accurate those are. My granny died after reading hers one day.

PETE: What?

JOHN: Mind you, she was 96. Doctor said her age had nothing to do with it, but I read them and it said for all Librans it was an auspicious day to take a long journey. I suppose you can't go on a longer one than death really . . .

(All exit.)

Scene 8

(Enter MARY.)

MARY: It's just finished, our meeting with management. They wanted 80 redundancies. They told us all their problems, how they had to rationalise here at MEL's. It's part of the programme, they said. And we said simply it wasn't on. Stalemate. We asked why we had to take nearly 18 per cent redundancies, and Bailey replied that they had already fought the GEC planners to get it as low as that. We walked out. Pete came into his own. He had all the fire, inspired the other stewards too. I stayed quiet.

(Enter PETE, PAT and JOHN, all laughing.)

PETE: That should give them something to think about, Mary.

MARY: Bailey will be on the phone all weekend.

JOHN: I hope he enjoys himself. I'll enjoy the Derby match twice as much if I know he's working.

PAT: So what happened when you walked out?

PETE: Nothing really. It was a good feeling though, you could see the fear in their eyes. It was as though we'd told them they were sacked.

PAT: What about the overtime ban?

PETE: We'll put it to the mass meeting Monday, with their proposals.

MARY: It's touch and go over any definite action apart from the ban though.

PETE: We'll sort that out at the meeting. I'm confident we can pull it off.

JOHN: Tell Pat how you went in. This is true, Pat, the ten stewards waltzed into the room with Pete singing at the top of his voice 'Take my hand, I'm a stranger in paradise'.

PAT: You haven't forgotten the blacking.

PETE: Albert from Stores told them that if anything more came from Automat we'd be out. They claimed to know nothing about it, said it must be an administrative error. They'll look into it.

JOHN: But how will we stop them if they ignore us and try to force through the redundancies?

PETE: Well, we'll wait till they sack you, then we'll take over the factory and live happily ever after.

(All laugh at perturbed JOHN.)

JOHN: Seriously.

PETE: Some of us are going to have a chat with some of the stewards from the AEI factories in the Park. I've got a feeling they'll be calling for redundancies there too – we could work out some joint action. That should put the fear of God into Bailey's lot.

JOHN: You're full of yourself, aren't you?

PETE: After winning you over, taking on a multinational like GEC should be a piece of cake.

JOHN: That's all right then.

(He's unaware of joke, others smile.)

PETE: And we think we've found the Trumid man.

PAT: At last.

PETE: We think it's one of the aspiring draughtsmen. The TASS steward, Dave, found him pinning up red scare bulletins in the toilets in the offices.

JOHN: A job for the Stretford Enders, is it?

PETE: No, Dave's been arguing him round.

JOHN: I thought it would be an office man.

PETE: You might know him, he's a devout Catholic.

JOHN (crosses himself): They're never infiltrating the Church as well.

(He exits.)

(MARY, PETE and PAT come out in turn to speak to audience in line.)

MARY: I thought I left those wartime caverns 30 years ago. In some ways I don't think I ever did. All those years, what for? So I can get a bungalow in St Anne's? I suppose I missed out not having a family but I don't really regret that. The redundancies might not go through but I'll wait until the next time. It will be a release when it does come. I can leave this cavern above ground forever. I only wish I didn't have to leave so much of myself here too. I'm part of this place. Just like the machines. I might leave it but it will never leave me. Pathetic, isn't it. My whole life just a cog in a machine.

(MARY walks offstage and through audience to leave.)

PAT: I was a mother when I was 4. That was when I got my first doll. I was a wife at 19 and a year later I exchanged my doll for the real thing. I didn't notice the difference much at first. Except for the noise, him crying all night. Being at home all day I hardly saw or spoke to anyone. It got so I was frightened to have Tom even touch me. Well, I didn't know who he wanted to make love to. Me?

Then I came to work here. Well, we needed the money. I became Pat Watts, clock number 329. It's funny but I'm happier working in this hell hole. At least here I'm someone. At home I felt like no one. Because working here I realised I'm no more a wife or mother than I am clock number 329. So many labels in the supermarket, what's the special offer this week? So I'm going to fight to keep my job, because surely I am not just a cog in their machine?

(PAT *exits to rear of set.*)

PETE: I was born when we 'never had it so good'. Brought up on Cow and Gate and grew up with a telly in the corner showing me all the world had to offer. From *Muffin the Mule* to *Take Your Pick*. I passed through school without much trouble. It was a bit like a prison sentence. Always being good with my hands I progressed quickly from my meccano set to engineering. I exchanged my *Hotspur* for the *Sun*. I was a man. Destined to work here at MEL's. The Beatles might have taken me to Penny Lane and Strawberry Fields but the 53 bus always took me back to Longsight. Is that what it's all about? The day to day grind? No, I wanted a good time, for me the discos and Boddington's bitter until I was legless. Then one day it clicked. From Cow and Gate to Boddington's didn't seem such a long way to have come. I realised I wanted more out of life. And I've spent the last few years trying to work out just what that 'more' is. I am not sure but I know that I wasn't born to spend my life here. That's why every day I fight MEL's management. It's not just a question of tackling them over productivity or redundancies or whatever else they come up with. For me, us, it's a struggle for survival. And somehow that battle makes me feel more real. Yes, it's a battle because they think we're just cogs in their machine.

(PETE *drifts offstage as* JOHN *bursts through from the backdrop to attack the audience for the last time.*)

JOHN: I've cracked it at last! I've got the loan of a fork-lift truck. I found a break in the fencing at the back of the car park. Pete's got his old van standing by. The security guards are having a brew so I'll have at least ten minutes to get it to the fence. THE SPANNER! I reckon I'll have enough orders after people see it in Ged's garden to keep me in beer money till Easter. I thought seriously about getting some cards printed. 'John Fitzpatrick Spanner Maker Supreme'. Hey, any of you out there want one? They could become very valuable in time. Collectors' items. I could even try and sell one to the Whitworth Gallery. No matter what happens, life goes on, doesn't it? And what more could I ask for? United always bubbling around the middle of the First Division. The spanner trade going from strength to strength. Perhaps I'll even change the design of the garden seat. You see I've got this dream of making a gigantic 28-foot cog next. Well, it will be Just a Cog cum . . . Just a Cog . . . cum . . . Well, it will be Just a Cog. God bless.

(JOHN exits happy, hands in pockets.)

Partisans

The play is set in the Solo Diecast factory, a small subsidiary of Chrysler Motors UK in Manchester, which is threatened with a takeover by the French car manufacturer Peugeot. It is 1978, the year the play was written. At the beginning of the play, the action flashes forward to when the factory is being occupied.

Characters

MOLE: So named because although he leaves the factory every evening by the main gate, he spends as much time as he can digging a tunnel out of the factory from behind his lathe.

BIRDMAN: Recently joined the factory after leaving one of Her Majesty's prisons.

HAMMER: Shop steward. She spends her time trying to bring the other characters together to act in their common interest.

FERRY: As in 'ferry 'cross the Mersey, Mersey Tunnel, mouth as wide as', a former militant, on anti-depressants.

WOMAN PATIENT: Remembers better days at the hospital.

HOSPITAL PORTER: Is hoping the corpses in the corridors will draw attention to hospital underfunding.

DOCTOR: Diagnoses strikes as the British disease and cannot prescribe for Greed.

Scene 1

(Sound of breaking glass, offstage. We are in the corner of a dark room lit by a single barred window. There is a row of lockers to the side. MOLE *enters, carrying a wooden club. As he passes the window* BIRDMAN *shines a torch in his face.)*

MOLE: The switch is by the window!

BIRDMAN: What are you whispering for?

HAMMER *(entering from opposite side)*: Come on, the sooner we get settled in here, we can find out how the others are doing at the hospital.

MOLE: After the dark, let there be light!

(The lights are turned on, and we see MOLE *turning away from the wall after he has flicked on the light switch.* MOLE *looks pleased with himself. There is a loud whistle, and* MOLE *looks through the window.)*

BIRDMAN: Hey, come over here, quick. *(He pulls* MOLE *down away from window, and faces door with a club raised over his head.* MOLE *and* HAMMER *duck back behind him in alarm.)*

(Enter FERRY *wearing a suit, carrying a television by the handle.)*

FERRY: If I'd have known, I'd have got dressed up. *(Points to television.)* Telly, and there's more gear outside as well.

*(*MOLE *and* BIRDMAN *exit, as* FERRY *moves further into the room and puts down the television.)*

HAMMER *(to audience)*: And this is where our story ends.

(Call offstage: Arrows!*)*

HAMMER *(to audience)*: Or begins. It's been just over a week since the notice of closure.

BIRDMAN *(enters carrying large can of beer)*: Beer!

HAMMER *(to audience)*: We've been living with the fear of it for months. We had written assurance from management that 'the firm will be in no way affected by the takeover'.

FERRY: Telly!

HAMMER *(to audience)*: I suppose they thought the talks at national level would soothe any doubts we had about their intentions, or else hope we were so divided amongst ourselves that *their* unity would win out.

(The three men call out, overlapping.)

MOLE: Arrows!

BIRDMAN: Beer!

FERRY: Telly!

FERRY: Telly!

MOLE: Arrows!

ALL THREE: Beer!

HAMMER: Sleeping bags!

(Exit MOLE.)

BIRDMAN and FERRY *(together)*: Sleeping bags!!

FERRY *(addressing audience)*: Well, what did they think we'd do? Hold out our hands while they sprinkled a few gold watches? £2000 if you'd worked here for 30 years, 360 quid to most of us. And then we'd joyfully go down the road and join the queue for our giros?

BIRDMAN: At the beginning that's exactly what you said we should do.

FERRY: Well, a lot's happened since then. Telly!

BIRDMAN *(addressing audience)*: I wondered why they started me. I'd only been here three months before all this. I suppose they thought if they're still taking people on it would look as though everything was all right. Must have been simpler to plan my employment and redundancy at the same time.

(FERRY *crosses behind* BIRDMAN, *to reach up for something beside* MOLE, *who is on a stepladder.*)

MOLE (*bending down from stepladder to shout at* FERRY): Beware of cobra licks!!

FERRY: The mole speaks!

MOLE: Before it bites, the cobra flashes out its tongue and gently licks and caresses its prey to a false sense of security.

FERRY (*to* BIRDMAN): Mr Cobra, used to be Works Manager years ago.

MOLE: Before sinking its teeth into its victim, paralysing it, and swallowing it whole!

(FERRY *and* BIRDMAN *look at each other.*)

FERRY (*points up*): Arrows!

BIRDMAN (*points down*): Beer!

FERRY: Beer?

MOLE: Telly!

BIRDMAN: Arrows!

MOLE: Beer!

BIRDMAN: Beer!

FERRY: T!

MOLE: B!

BIRDMAN: A!

FERRY: B

BIRDMAN: T

MOLE: A

MOLE and BIRDMAN: Beer!

HAMMER *(joins men)*: Duplicating ink!

(BIRDMAN moves away with a click of his finger. FERRY turns away. MOLE exits.)

(Spotlight on HAMMER.)

HAMMER *(reading from newspaper)*: 'Solo Diecast is to close. This has been confirmed by the Paris headquarters of Peugeot Citröen, whose recent takeover of Chrysler UK has now sealed the fate of its component subsidiary based in Wythenshawe after earlier promises of survival. It will mean the loss of 150 jobs. The union has yet to make a statement.' *(Looks up.)* They told the papers before us. That was a shrewd move. When I read it for the first time, there was a feeling as though it'd already closed. Well, we still came to work though, nothing had really changed for us, but out there we were finished. Reading it in the paper made you half believe it yourself. It was a while before we did anything. They must have been relying on us to bury ourselves, and if it'd happened four months earlier, most of the stewards here would have been handing out the spades. *(Moves off.)*

FERRY *(turning back to face audience)*: Straightforward. Security's given out the keys, straightforward.

BIRDMAN: Shame about the Mole.

FERRY: He'll bounce back.

BIRDMAN: How long's he been working on it?

FERRY: About four months now, on and off.

BIRDMAN: Ironic.

HAMMER: How's this sound then? *(Clears throat and reads.)* 'As assurances given us by Solo's management about the continuation of all jobs and planning agreements have now been broken by our new owners, and negotiations at a local and national level have failed to secure our future, we have decided to protect our jobs by the occupation of Solo's. We will not allow the removal of any stock or machinery, and demand further talks to meet our demands.'

FERRY (*rolling eyes*): Amen!

HAMMER: Well, we've got to have something for the papers tomorrow.

FERRY (*taking piece of paper from HAMMER's hand*): Who wrote that?

HAMMER: All the stewards.

FERRY: It reads like it too. Look, we want something short and snappy.

HAMMER: Like?

FERRY: Stuff you! Up us!

BIRDMAN: Stuff you up us?

FERRY: Up us, stuff you? Doesn't read too bad when you look at it a second time, does it?

(*MOLE enters carrying a giant dice and looks around for somewhere to put it. BIRDMAN places a large square block in front of him, and he puts it down on it.*)

MOLE: Found it in the boardroom.

HAMMER: Must be part of their complex decision-making process.

FERRY: Executive toy.

BIRDMAN: What is it?

MOLE: They had this picture of it on the wall. (*Produces a framed painting of the dice and hangs it on backdrop.*)

FERRY: Oh, I recognise it now! It's the Chairman working late!

HAMMER: Oh! *(To dice.)* Well, this may come as a bit of a shock to you, but about the closure – I'm afraid things haven't quite gone as you planned.

MOLE *(hands on hips)*: We've taken over! What are you gonna do about it?

BIRDMAN: Hey, it's not speaking.

FERRY *(to dice)*: About my holiday pay ...

HAMMER: It could be French.

FERRY *(to dice)*: Avez-vous holiday pay?

MOLE *(shouting at dice)*: We're not going, we want our jobs back!

FERRY: He means it!

HAMMER: It is possible the closure had nothing to do with her.

FERRY: Her?

HAMMER: Anyway, there's nothing in the Rule Book about holding hostages.

BIRDMAN *(pulls a bit of paper from his pocket)*: It's got something about it here though: 'To start, roll dice ...'

FERRY: Hey, those are the rules to Mole's Monopoly set!

MOLE: It's not leaving here till we know which side it's on!

FERRY *(at MOLE)*: Aargh ...

MOLE: And we could do with a donation to the occupation fund. Search it – bound to be loaded!

FERRY: I wonder what day I'll be signing on. Come here Mole, I want to have a word with you.

(MOLE and FERRY exit.)

BIRDMAN: You going to try and get home tonight?

HAMMER *(writing on paper)*: I hadn't thought about it.

BIRDMAN: Yeah, it's hard to know what to do.

HAMMER: Settle in!

BIRDMAN: Oh, you're confident . . .

HAMMER *(looking up)*: For a woman?

BIRDMAN: Yeah, for a woman.

HAMMER: At least you admit it.

(Enter MOLE and FERRY, talking together, walking across stage.)

MOLE *(with arm on FERRY's shoulder, continuing conversation)*:
. . . And it's at those times you're most vulnerable.

FERRY: And you really believe O-levels did the trick for you,
then?

MOLE: Only on Wednesdays and Fridays.

*(MOLE and FERRY exit on the opposite side of stage from their
entrance.)*

BIRDMAN: What a summer!

HAMMER: Seems to be turning out quite well.

BIRDMAN: I never thought it would.

HAMMER: Well, you played your part in making sure it did, that's
what matters.

BIRDMAN: You know they could have sacked me any time, I never
even finished my probationary period.

HAMMER *(walking past him across stage)*: They had their sights
set on higher things. *(Hands him the paper she's been writing on, and
they stand together at one side of stage.)*

(MOLE and FERRY have entered again.)

MOLE: Everything's moving so fast, especially on Wednesdays and Fridays.

FERRY *(claps hands together, speaks to all)*: Come on, I know, let's uh – let's have a game of cards! Look, we could – we could play for the whole factory!

HAMMER: We already have.

FERRY: No look, we – we'll split it up into equal sections. By morning – all this could be mine ...

BIRDMAN: What would you do with it?

FERRY: Get rid of you lot for a start.

(MOLE and BIRDMAN look challengingly at him.)

FERRY: So serious, aren't you – Open the beer, get the telly on, let's have a game of darts. We'll probably be here for hours yet.

MOLE: Hours?

HAMMER: You're helpful.

FERRY: I'm here, what more do you want?

HAMMER: Are you?

BIRDMAN: Oh, we must give him credit for that.

MOLE: Against all the odds!

FERRY *(laughs)*: Birdman can talk! When he first started here he needed a lot of straightening out! And don't forget it was me that pushed you to be steward. *(Points at HAMMER.)* The Mole? *(Looks MOLE up and down.)* The Mole's the mole. Look, it's not easy for me throwing my life into this turmoil. I mean, years ago we had some roots. Then when Chryslers took over it went from bad to bad. And you remember Sid? Well, he was so confused he left here and joined British Leyland, and what kind of end is that for a toolmaker? We lost something along the line somewhere.

HAMMER: Listen to him. You're not on your own, you know. There's another 149 other lads involved as well.

BIRDMAN: And now we've occupied. (*Exits stage.*)

MOLE: It's only the beginning. (*Follows* BIRDMAN *offstage.*)

FERRY: Well, it seems to have taken a long time to get it started!

HAMMER: It took us a long time to get together.

(*Fade to black.*)

Scene 2

(*Flashback to before the occupation.* FERRY *and* HAMMER *are standing together in a well-lit room. She has her back to audience and arms crossed, he has hands in pockets, jacket off, and is facing audience.* MOLE *is standing behind a hardboard painted lathe/partition.*)

FERRY: Look, you'll do well, the T&G say they want women stewards.

HAMMER: I don't know, it's the time.

FERRY: Look, I'm behind you, the Mole's behind you. (*Laughs.*) He's as far behind you as you can get.

HAMMER: If this is some game...

MOLE: Don't take any notice of him, most of us want you.

HAMMER: Yeah? Nobody else'll do it then. (*Exits.*)

MOLE (*to* FERRY): You make me sick!

FERRY: Shut up and keep digging.

MOLE: You don't care about anybody, do you?

FERRY: Look, I think she's very attractive and if she tidies herself up a bit she should be fine, you know.

MOLE *(looking at* FERRY's *clothes)*: They say ties give away the personality.

FERRY: What's wrong with wanting to look smart? Anyway I've got to show the new boy around.

MOLE: How far did you have to crawl to get that job, eh?

FERRY: Not as far as I'll throw you! They wanted someone with personality.

MOLE: He must be part of the new expansion.

FERRY: Yeah, that makes three new starts this . . . year.

BIRDMAN *(enters singing)*: 'And he painted matchstick men and matchstick cats and dogs!' *(Looks around and takes off his coat.)*

FERRY: You must be the new boy – Personnel finished with you?

BIRDMAN: No, that's why I'm here.

FERRY: Yeah, well they told me to show you the ropes.

BIRDMAN: Doesn't matter, same old routine, I'll pick it up.

FERRY: They asked me to show you around.

BIRDMAN: I've heard it all before!

FERRY: Didn't they tell you about me, then?

BIRDMAN: Look, they told me it wasn't a closed shop, and there was no pressure on me to join the union if I didn't want to, no pressure at all. If I was against it on religious grounds, it was all right with them, it was my right not to join if I so desire, I have the law on my side, I mustn't feel pressurised in the slightest.

MOLE: What'd you say?

BIRDMAN: Nothing to them, but I thought I'd better join the union to stop the pressure on me not to join the union.

MOLE: They'll try anything.

FERRY: Look, this is the section where the bearings come from, they come down here . . .

BIRDMAN: Yeah, same old stuff. Hey, you know before they built all this, there was nothing here at all.

MOLE: I'm the Mole!

FERRY (*to* BIRDMAN): Are you coloured?

(HAMMER, *having re-entered, reaches over and smacks* FERRY *on the bottom with rolled-up paper.*)

FERRY (*jumping forward*): Ouch!

HAMMER (*to* BIRDMAN): So you're the expansion.

MOLE: All 33 per cent of it.

FERRY: He wants to join the union.

HAMMER: He'd better see George, he's the steward for this section.

MOLE: At the moment.

FERRY (*eyeing up* BIRDMAN): Looks Italian.

HAMMER: The Poet finished the second bulletin. (*Passes paper to* MOLE.)

FERRY (*to* BIRDMAN): It's a kind of works paper, set up by the stewards' committee. It keeps everyone informed, what's going on with the wage claim, safety and stuff. Management don't like it though, they say it's run by the reds.

BIRDMAN: We had one inside.

FERRY: Inside? Well, you'll meet The Poet. He's one of the old ones, they've been trying to get rid of him for years. He writes poems for the paper, that's why we call him The Poet. Management stole one of his best ones for their ad on TV, they changed it a bit. His one went . . . (*sings raucously*) 'Put a little Sunbeam in your life, and it'll wipe the smile off your face!' (*Addresses* BIRDMAN *directly*.) Inside? What, done a lot of inside work, have you?

BIRDMAN: Walton.

FERRY: Walton? Hey, that's a coincidence, Mole comes from Bootle. Walton Jail! (*Turns back to talk to* HAMMER *and* MOLE.) Lock up your valuables, he's a villain, been inside, that's where he got that suntan!

HAMMER (*having read paper*): I see Luton's put in for 15 per cent. We'll have to jack ours up a bit to match it, eh?

MOLE: That dispute's still on at Linwood.

BIRDMAN: Hey, look, I was born in Longsight and I served my time at Ward and Goldstone's as an electrical engineer. I worked there until I was arrested in my flat with some drugs that belonged to my flatmate. Spent 18 months in Walton, been out of work for the last three. And now I'm here, okay?

FERRY: Drugs!

HAMMER (*to* BIRDMAN): I'm the Hammer, they call me that because I nearly put one across that idiot's head for getting me worked up the same way you are now. I was an arresting baby girl and I've been serving a continuous 27-year sentence ever since. Pleased to meet you. Go and get George to sign you up.

(BIRDMAN *picks up coat and brushes past* FERRY *as he leaves*.)

FERRY: Everything's fine with me, man!

(BIRDMAN *exits*.)

FERRY: Did you see his eyes? He was as high as a kite!

HAMMER: Why don't you get some work done?

MOLE: Two-faced.

FERRY: Look, there's one and a half million on the dole, and they're giving jobs to people like that?

HAMMER: He's skilled.

FERRY: I'm sure he is, it's what at that's worrying me.

MOLE (*pointing to paper*): Well, here's something that might interest you – those rumours about closing Linwood . . .

FERRY (*snatching paper from MOLE*): God, the selfish sods! The cheek of it, asking us for support! Well, if they carry on like this Chrysler's will close them down, and where does that leave us, eh?

HAMMER: Up to our ears in splanges.

FERRY: Oh, it's all right for the Scotch – they're Scotch. We'll be left with nothing.

HAMMER: It's only rumours.

MOLE: They wouldn't close it down.

FERRY: Oh, but look, I see there's a ray of light for you two here – they've declared workers' control!

(*MOLE and HAMMER lean together to look at paper.*)

FERRY: In a mental hospital in Surrey.

(*MOLE and HAMMER look at him.*)

(*Fade to black.*)

(*As lights come up again, BIRDMAN is putting coat away in locker, FERRY is talking to him.*)

FERRY: First impressions, I didn't mean anything by it.

BIRDMAN: I'll forgive you.

FERRY: Well, once you explained.

BIRDMAN (*turning to face him*): Have to do a lot of that, will I?

FERRY: Still having treatment?

BIRDMAN: Do you go to night school for it?

FERRY: What?

BIRDMAN: City and Guilds in getting up people's noses?

FERRY: I'm just trying to break the ice.

BIRDMAN: Look, I don't have to explain myself to you or anyone else, okay?

FERRY: There's a lot more to working here than clocking on, doing your work and clocking off.

BIRDMAN: I was under the impression that's what they paid me for.

FERRY: I don't want to know your life story.

BIRDMAN: You've had it already!

FERRY: We've got to work on this section together.

BIRDMAN: Work? That's what I've been trying to do!

FERRY: It'll take a while to settle down.

BIRDMAN: If I'm here that long. (*Sits down with newspaper.*)

FERRY: Oh, just passing through, then?

BIRDMAN: This isn't my trade.

FERRY: A tradesman! I get it, just a stop-gap is it here, before Saudi Arabia, Libya, Walsall?

BIRDMAN: Maybe.

FERRY: Nice place, Walsall.

BIRDMAN (*looks up from newspaper*): Hey, why'd you call him the Mole?

FERRY: It's what he is.

BIRDMAN: A mole?

FERRY: He digs. You know what? You might be able to help him.

He'd really appreciate that. *(Goes over to painted lathe in corner, leans over edge, shouts very loudly.)* Mo-o-o-ole!

BIRDMAN: What are you doing?

FERRY: Bringing him up. *(Shouts very loudly over hardboard lathe again.)* Mole! It's me, Ferry!

MOLE *(shouting from below, in his tunnel)*: What do you want?

FERRY: I've got the Birdman of Alcatraz here, he might have a few tips for you.

BIRDMAN: Where is he?

FERRY: He's down his tunnel.

BIRDMAN: Tunnel?

FERRY: Must be four months now, yeah?

BIRDMAN *(comes over to painted lathe)*: You mean he really is down a tunnel?

FERRY: All his own work!

BIRDMAN: I thought he worked on this lathe.

FERRY: This? *(Knocks on painted lathe.)* This is just a bit of hardboard. He's dismantled the real one and uses it to prop up his tunnel.

BIRDMAN: What about his work?

FERRY: The tunnel?

BIRDMAN: Splanges!

FERRY: The rest of us cover for him, I've told you there's more to working here than clocking on and off.

(BIRDMAN peers over painted lathe as if looking down a deep hole.)

FERRY *(shouts over painted lathe again)*: Hey, Mole! Are you coming? *(Looks at watch and continues to shout down hole.)* Anyway it's tea-break, we've warned you about working straight through!

BIRDMAN: But what's it for?

FERRY: He did explain it to me once, but I never really grasped it. It's all to do with his escape.

BIRDMAN: Escape? Don't they let him out?

FERRY: Of course! How else do you think he gets rid of the rubble? Every night he loads up the boot of his old Anglia. I've warned him though, it's ruining the suspension on it, look. (*Peers out of the window.*)

BIRDMAN: If he goes home every night, what's he digging a tunnel for?

FERRY: It's all to do with iron bars do not a prison make. I bet you said a lot of that in Walton, eh? And 'mind-forged manacles', all that stuff, very complex. He'll tell you all about it.

BIRDMAN: Haven't the management noticed?

FERRY: Well, the foreman is regularly physically intimidated, and they say that the last time a manager was seen down on our section it was to announce sixpence off the rate and ask us to put our backs behind the war effort. Boer War, it was.

(*MOLE is banging from behind lathe.*)

FERRY (*pointing at BIRDMAN*): But only those in our section know about it!

MOLE (*shouting roughly*): Come on! Give us a hand.

(*BIRDMAN stands behind the painted lathe and pulls MOLE up. MOLE is wearing a balaclava and goggles, and has various digging things strapped around his chest. He stands for a moment peering upwards, away from BIRDMAN now behind him.*)

MOLE (*breathes out heavily, as if catching his breath, and takes his goggles off*): Not long now.

(*MOLE starts to dust himself off, and after a moment BIRDMAN begins to help him, dusting hard at* MOLE's *trousers as* MOLE *bends over, cleaning himself.)*

FERRY: He takes visitors down on Wednesdays and Fridays!

*(*MOLE *stops what he's doing and looks back to see* BIRDMAN.*)*

FERRY: It's an amazing feeling, not so much being down it, but coming up.

MOLE *(turns back to* FERRY*)*: Shut it, will you!

FERRY: I've just been singing your praises to Birdman, Mole. Hey, Mole, meet Birdman.

BIRDMAN: I didn't believe him.

MOLE: You should, everything he says comes straight from the heart, it's in his locker.

FERRY: I wondered where I'd left it.

BIRDMAN: About your tunnel . . . *(Takes hold of* MOLE's *arm.)*

MOLE *(pushes him away)*: It's a secret, I suppose he told you that?

BIRDMAN: I won't say a word!

FERRY: I had to swear the Water Buffalo Oath. Had to promise I'd never eat another Wimpy.

*(*BIRDMAN *crosses over to* FERRY, *picks up the newspaper once more.* MOLE *walks behind them and exits.)*

FERRY: What that's got to do with animals, I'll never know.

HAMMER *(enters from other side of* FERRY *and pushes him off the seat)*: Move.

FERRY: That's why we voted her steward. Straight in, knows what she wants, gets it.

HAMMER: Just give me five minutes' peace, okay?

FERRY: Clear-headed even under pressure, she . . .

BIRDMAN: She said to leave her alone!

FERRY: What's it got to do with you?

HAMMER *(to BIRDMAN)*: I look after myself; handling him is the least of my problems. I don't need your help.

(BIRDMAN goes back to reading paper, HAMMER stares into distance. FERRY taps back of BIRDMAN's newspaper.)

FERRY: Mid-day edition, goes out for dinner! *(to HAMMER)* Not keen on the trough, then? Still looking for jobs in the Emerald Isles? Well . . . *(Snatches section of newspaper.)* I'll just borrow the news section to read, while I relieve myself of any further responsibility to you. *(Tucks paper under arm, and exits, watched by BIRDMAN.)*

BIRDMAN: Met some blokes in my time, but him? Talk? He never stops. I tell you, if he keeps on my back I'll put one on him!

HAMMER: Handsome though, isn't he?

(BIRDMAN turns away.)

HAMMER: Offended you as well, have I? It's all part of the unplanned initiation. It helps to find out who you are, what you're like.

BIRDMAN: What the hell's it got to do with any of you lot?

HAMMER: It's a small factory, you get to know everyone. It's very important.

(FERRY shouts out from offstage: 'Sod off, I'm in here!!')

HAMMER: And when the extractor fan blows the air in, you can catch the smell from the toilets as well. But I suppose you're used to that aren't you, working closely with people, someone with your experience?

BIRDMAN: First him, now you? Well, you can stick your initiation, I've had enough of watching what I say, who I say it to. I thought there were some nutters inside, but here? Digging tunnels when they go home every night, strangers on your back nagging you? You're worse than the screws! And a steward called Hammer who's a . . .

HAMMER: Woman?

BIRDMAN: If you like! I've had enough of this, I'm jacking. (*Begins to exit.*)

HAMMER (*stands and moves to centre of room*): That's a surprise. I wouldn't have thought someone who, as I heard it, had 'seen it all before, same old routine', knew it all . . . it wouldn't be enough to make him jack it in!

(*MOLE enters and stands between them.*)

MOLE: By my calculations I should come up next to the hospital laundry. Miss that fencing by about three foot this side of the mortuary. Hey, it'll have to be accurate though, otherwise I'll come up right in it, then I'll be leaving a dead and alive hole for a dead and dead one! (*Turns to BIRDMAN.*) Do you think you could give me a hand getting some rubble into the back of my car?

HAMMER: Forget it, Mole, you're too late. He's had enough, he's leaving.

MOLE: Leaving? He's only just started! (*Goes over to BIRDMAN, who is still standing by door as if about to exit.*) Anyway, he can't leave, he's Birdman. (*BIRDMAN and MOLE look back towards HAMMER.*)

(*Fade to black.*)

Scene 3

(*MOLE is standing behind lathe, FERRY has his back to him, pacing agitatedly up and down.*)

FERRY: I'll have to go down to the hospital, you know, this news about the strikes only confirms it for me.

MOLE: How long you been on them?

FERRY: Six months.

MOLE: Why don't you get a hobby?

FERRY: Hobby?

MOLE: Helps you relax.

FERRY: Another tunnel and the floor will give way!

MOLE: This isn't a hobby!

FERRY: I know.

MOLE: What you on now, then?

FERRY: Six a day. They're only mild ones though.

MOLE: Valium?

FERRY: I'll only be gone for the afternoon.

MOLE: Ask Birdman, he might be able to help.

FERRY (*turning to* MOLE *violently*): You mention a word of this to anyone . . . I'm warning you, Mole!

MOLE: I'll get Hammer to raise it at the Branch. Dear T&G, Brother Ferry of our section is going nuts!

FERRY: I'm telling you!

MOLE: Is that why you packed in being a steward?

FERRY: After the last pay negotiations, yeah.

MOLE: At least you're fully qualified for that Supervisor's job now, eh?

FERRY (*just realises*): Linwood. I went to the last big national stewards' meeting, you know, just before Chrysler said they'd chuck it in unless they got the government money. Do you know, those Jock stewards actually got up at the meeting and said that if they got the contract to build the new Sunbeam they'd make the car with little sporrans on!

MOLE: They were probably joking.

FERRY: Yeah, well, no wonder Chrysler wants to close them down.

MOLE: Wonder how it'll affect us?

FERRY: God knows.

MOLE: When have you got to go to the hospital, then?

FERRY (*looking at watch*): Soon.

(*HAMMER enters and leans on MOLE's lathe.*)

MOLE: What's the news from the front line?

HAMMER: Still only rumours. I don't see how they think they can get away with it, closing Linwood down. Well, Coventry and Luton would come out and that'd cripple them.

MOLE: They've been blackmailing us long enough about pulling out.

HAMMER: Government would never allow it.

FERRY: Give us to British Leyland.

HAMMER: It's hard being out on a limb here.

MOLE: 150 of us is a big limb though.

HAMMER: But they might try and lay us off and then close them down, see?

FERRY: Look, surely those Jocks know there's no way they can get more money!

HAMMER: It's nothing to do with money.

FERRY: Perhaps they're on strike to get the little sporrans put on.

HAMMER: Sporrans?

FERRY (*daydreaming*): Painting them tartan, I tell you the World Cup's gone to their heads!

HAMMER: It's the supervisors.

FERRY: You see? Up there even the company men are union men, it's in their blood.

HAMMER: From what we heard, management have provoked the strike to cover up for not ordering enough raw materials.

FERRY: But we've got storerooms full of splanges here!

HAMMER: Exactly! They're not up there, they're down here, whose fault's that?

MOLE: What are we going to do about it?

HAMMER: We'll have to see.

FERRY (*in reverie*): The old Humber Super Snipe – now there was a car. I used to have a Dinky of it. I always wanted one. Craftsman-worked, built like a tank, built in England, I mean who did you ever know was in their right mind when they bought a Hillman Imp?

MOLE: What are you talking about?

FERRY: Chrysler haven't done too bad. The Avenger's not a bad car. Trouble is you can't get hold of them for love nor money. Why? Made in Scotland!

HAMMER: You were going to buy ten, were you? Out of your overtime?

FERRY: With my money you must be joking, but it's a good car.

HAMMER: Who cares what cars they make, it's more money we should be fighting for – that's why you voted me steward. Every stewards' meeting I go to, I come out with some management problem to solve. All they see us as is a way of organising production for them. It's crazy all right! Maybe Linwood aren't half as crazy as us, eh? Perhaps we could learn something from them! Now it's our jobs at stake as well, perhaps we'll get our priorities right again.

FERRY: Look who she's talking to about money!

MOLE: What did the other stewards say?

HAMMER: I think we should call a mass meeting, find out what the shop floor make of this mess.

FERRY: Shop floor won't thank you for that.

HAMMER: I don't want thanks, I'm just doing what I think's best, okay?

FERRY: And you're the first?

HAMMER: No, I never said I was.

FERRY: In the end it'll swamp you too. I seem to remember tramping up the same garden path myself.

MOLE: Haven't you got somewhere to go this afternoon?

FERRY: Yeah, that's right. (*Turns to go.*)

HAMMER: That's convenient for you.

MOLE: No, he's got to go to the dentist's.

FERRY: Chiropodist's. (*Says this at the same time as* MOLE *says* 'dentist's'.)

FERRY: The chiropodist's on my way to the dentist's. Got a slight touch of foot and mouth, you know?

(*Exit* FERRY.)

HAMMER: Why do you let him get away like that? Planning escapes for everyone now?

MOLE: I was just trying to calm things down a bit – there's no point arguing with him, you know what he's like.

HAMMER: Not worth bothering with, eh?

MOLE: No.

HAMMER: Well, he could be right, then!

MOLE: Yeah – no, he's worth bothering with, it's just that I knew he wanted to get off. Listen – mass meeting, more money, good idea! Do it if you want to! *(MOLE disappears behind the lathe.)*

HAMMER: Let me know when you get through.

MOLE *(reappearing above lathe)*: Tunnel? *(Proudly.)* Not long now.

HAMMER: I might want to come with you.

(Fade to black – MOLE is spotlit.)

MOLE *(to audience)*: Eight months now, graft! But it will be worth it, 'cos it's no good if they get you in here. *(Taps head.)* Look at Ferry, they got him. Most of them here, not me, I've got it all planned. They won't break me! I built my own way out. All my own work! Won't use it till it's necessary, but it's there, nearly ready, not long to go now. For when I need it. I started small-scale ones at school. I was escaping from the Germans then, Gestapo, and PE. The number of times I got battered by my mates for reading *The Eagle*. They won't get me though, not in here, I've got my escape all planned.

(Fade to black.)

Scene 4

(The lockers have been turned round; their other side shows a sign 'Ward C6' over a doorway. The lathe has been reversed too, and we now see a hospital bed with a body on it covered by a sheet.)

(*FERRY enters and looks around, looks at watch.*)

FERRY: Don't like coming here. Hospitals make me feel ill. But my doctor's here Wednesday afternoon, so it's more convenient popping over. It being next door. Very close. Right on top of us. It suits him, anyway. (*Looks around.*) Eh? (*Bends down to hospital bed.*) What's that? You're a private patient, you shouldn't be treated like this? No! Shame. What's the matter with you, then? You own a chemical firm making starch, yeah? Arguing over safety? And they threw you in the mix? Christ, that's a bit stiff, innit? (*FERRY taps the hardboard bed loudly.*) So are you! Well, don't worry, I am sure someone will be along in a minute to chip you out. (*Moves forwards and talks to audience again.*) And if I know the NUPE lot in here, they'll check on him in a . . . fortnight. Well, they've had a lot of problems here. I used to hear all about it at the Trades Council. Not enough staff, waiting list as long as your arm. Probably why Stiff there's in the corridor, waiting for a bed or a shelf somewhere. Not enough staff, place is packed. I heard they're closing it down.

WOMAN PATIENT (*appears from behind hospital bed, leans forward, shouts*): You been waiting long?

FERRY: No, I've an appointment, actually.

WOMAN PATIENT: That doesn't mean a thing! (*Moves out and takes his arm.*) You know, years ago, I can remember when you'd spend a whole day going around the hospital. Casualty, X-ray, back to Casualty again. Have a meal in the canteen, read the papers, have a chat, share your troubles. It's all different now! They don't want patients! Come here needing anything less than open heart surgery, and you feel you're putting them out! It's all changed. Used to be a full day, and you'd find somebody that was worth talking to. One day I went and I met this man, about 40, very clean, and he'd caught his testicles in the Hoover – well, you don't like to ask, you know – and they'd blown up the size of a football! Well, one had – painful – made me eyes water just to look at him. Funny thing was, they wouldn't send an ambulance – no! They made him take the bus. He got thrown off four times and arrested twice. Suppose they thought – well, you know. In the end all they did was bandage him up and send him home, told him not to do anything strenuous. *(She turns to go.)* I blame the Labour government myself. *(Exit, whistling.)*

FERRY: I could do with a tablet. *(Moves to side of stage.)*

(There is a banging from opposite side of stage.)

HOSPITAL PORTER *(leans over and shouts to hospital bed)*: Someone will see you shortly! *(Raises hand and points to FERRY.)* Ferry?

(FERRY looks around.)

HOSPITAL PORTER: Haven't seen you on the Trades Council lately!

FERRY: No, I've given up – about six months ago, actually.

HOSPITAL PORTER: It's all happening here, reaching the point of no return! Boiling point has been reached! Both sides, we know who's to blame. We are taking steps!

FERRY: Yeah, I read all about it!

HOSPITAL PORTER: No point in believing all you read!

FERRY: Not all of it, just the rumours I suppose.

HOSPITAL PORTER: We'll be calling on you for support, substantial!

FERRY: I don't deal with that side of it any more.

HOSPITAL PORTER: Only two sides.

FERRY: Well, it's just that we've got a lot of problems –

HOSPITAL PORTER: We've all got problems.

FERRY: It's just that –

HOSPITAL PORTER: Corpses are piling up!

FERRY: Eh?

HOSPITAL PORTER: Soon we won't be able to move for stiffs!

FERRY: Oh, what, him back —

HOSPITAL PORTER: Selective overtime ban in the mortuary. It's really beginning to bite on the corpses. The administration won't like it – another two weeks and that'll make them see sense. We'll have every corridor filled with them. People will complain. It'll bring it to their attention, ram the implications home. Death gives a hospital a bad name. Something's got to give! We'll be in touch! *(Exits.)*

FERRY *(wandering back to the other side of the stage, where a DOCTOR has emerged and is edging along a ledge by the back wall)*: Yeah, just half a tablet and I really think I'd be all right.

DOCTOR: Next! Hello, Mr Thompson, everything okay? *(Reaches into pocket.)* Fine, here's your prescription!

FERRY: Fine, fine. I wondered if um . . .

DOCTOR: Working is it? The treatment?

FERRY: Could you up the dose a bit?

DOCTOR: Not working?

FERRY: Well, it is, it's just that, um . . .

DOCTOR: How's work now, still a problem?

FERRY: It's all right, a lot of problems but . . .

DOCTOR: No sense in holding on to them.

FERRY: No, I haven't, I've let it all go, but it's a strain, you know.

DOCTOR: Just work?

FERRY: I dunno.

DOCTOR: It can't help, working in that environment!

FERRY: We got this new extractor fan –

DOCTOR: Strikes! The British disease!

FERRY: Disease?

DOCTOR: Rife here too, I'm afraid, last place you'd think you'd see it fester.

FERRY: No, it's not that, the last strike we had was ages ago . . .

DOCTOR: Of course, Greed is something we can't, alas, give tablets for!

FERRY: Who said anything about greed?

DOCTOR: The British disease! (*He continues to sidle around the ledge at the edge of the room, and exits through the doorway.*)

(*Spotlight on* FERRY, *all else fades.*)

FERRY (*to audience*): Greed? Disease? Greed? What greed? Greedy about what? All I wanted was more money to pay the bills that were going up all the time – I've worked for it! But I felt I was. In my nightmares I was greedy though, very greedy. Not at first. At first I was frightened, scared, terrified! People were pointing me out in the street as I walked along – 'There goes Greedy', they'd chant. I'd say 'No! I've worked for it!', but it would be in the papers, on the television, they'd have me chained up, shouting – 'Greedy, greedy, greedy – you want another £5 a week?' 'Yeah!' 'Greedy!'

(FERRY *falls to his knees.*)

I used to crawl along in the gutters to avoid eye contact, but they'd still shout out at me – 'Greedy!' they'd shout. I thought, 'Right – greedy am I? Yeah!' – I stood up!

(FERRY *rises from the floor.*)

Me! Nutter! Hate the rich! Envy them! Want what they've got – everything! Do you know I felt taller? I went to work as though nothing had happened, but I knew I was different. I'd become

– Greedy! There was an ache in my stomach as I clocked on. Oh, it felt huge, cavernous, empty, not filled, by now I was well and truly – Greedy! The section seemed normal, but I knew I was not. I took my place at my machine, and the ache in my stomach turned to desire – physical requirement – greed! And then . . . and then he came closer . . . In my mind I begged him not to, not him, not . . . the foreman! He was against the wage claim from the beginning. His hand rose, his finger pointed – 'You're Greedy!' he shouted. It happened so fast and the gnawing in my stomach forced my mouth open wider and wider! 'Greedy!' he said, and I thought 'Yes, I AM! – And I bit off his arm! 'He's bit off my arm', he cried, but the taste only whetted my appetite, and in one gulp he went down! I had eaten the foreman! He was 'armless but tasty. The Production Manager ran up – 'You, Greedy!' That was my cue – one slurp, he was down . . . I licked his wallet as it passed down – he only had £3 in it and an ASTMS membership card. For a second I thought I'd made a terrible mistake, but it was too late, I grew bigger and bigger as the whole of management lined up in chorus shouting 'Greedy!' 'Yeah, Greedy here!' and I ate the lot of them! I was huge, filling up, but Greedy! Chrysler's Head Office came down, the union Executive – then there was police, dogs! Marksmen! And I flicked them onto the back of my throat with my tongue! Old age pensioners, clutching their tins of salmon, screaming 'Greedy!' 'Yeah, Greedy here!' and I ate them too! Television next, and they all came, and I ate them all!

(FERRY *finally bends over, clutching his stomach.*)

But by now I was full . . . Full. Full. Eh? (*Hears noise coming from the hospital bed and shouts back to it.*) Someone will be along in a minute to chip you out.

(*Fade to black.*)

Scene 5

(Lockers etc. turned round to their original positions. Back at the factory. BIRDMAN *is leaning over* MOLE'*s lathe, looking down the hole and speaking to him.)*

MOLE *(muffled voice)*: Solo Diecast.

BIRDMAN *(straining to hear)*: You what?

MOLE *(rises up from the hole carrying bag of rubble and puts it down in the middle of the room)*: Solo Diecast used to be part of British Light Steel Pressings, which was taken over by Rootes years ago. Then Chrysler took them over, and that's how it ended up. It's just a small family firm.

BIRDMAN *(examining hole)*: Do you get on with Ferry?

MOLE: He's all right.

BIRDMAN: Why do you call him Ferry?

MOLE *(lying down on the ground, reclining, using his body to measure distance above ground along the floor)*: He was the first one to call me Mole – that was when he was still a steward, mind.

BIRDMAN: Him?

MOLE: Oh yeah, they say he was red hot. Well, hot. He'd talk rings around anyone.

BIRDMAN: He's got a mouth on him.

MOLE *(propels himself, on his back, across the room to the wall and then stops measuring, looking dissatisfied)*: That's where it comes from – Ferry – 'Ferry 'cross the Mersey, Mersey Tunnel, mouth as wide as.' I gave it to him.

BIRDMAN: Yeah? Why'd he give it up?

MOLE *(getting up)*: What?

BIRDMAN: Being a steward!

MOLE: Oh, that was after the last pay claim. Ferry went out on a limb. We couldn't break the pay code and Ferry wanted to stick out for another £10. Well, most of the stewards backed down. Afterwards union officials came down and said it was for the best, so he jacked it in.

BIRDMAN: But he's always calling us for asking for more money.

MOLE: Yeah, he's a bit like that.

BIRDMAN: Is he National Front?

MOLE: Ferry?

BIRDMAN: He was asking me if I was coloured!

MOLE: There used to be a couple of NF here, he was always going for them. Bit of a patriot though.

BIRDMAN: Doesn't like the Scotch.

MOLE: Doesn't like anyone much.

BIRDMAN: Hammer said it was like joining a football team, working here.

MOLE: Did she? I don't play myself.

(*HAMMER enters.*)

HAMMER: They couldn't organise. It's like wading through mud. 'We'll have to see what they say,' 'Take our time over this one,' 'Mustn't be too hasty putting jobs in jeopardy.'

BIRDMAN: Hitting management hard, Hammer?

HAMMER: Management? That's the stewards' meeting. Half of them reach for their pension books the minute you mention you should do anything.

MOLE: About what?

HAMMER: Anything. Support for Linwood, new pay claim. I can see now why Ferry pushed me for the job. It was his way of getting his own back after me hounding him over the last wage claim when he was steward.

BIRDMAN: I still can't see him as a steward.

MOLE (to HAMMER): He thought he was a Nazi!

HAMMER: Ferry? He's too soft! We used to have a couple here. Why, are you one, then?

BIRDMAN: Yeah, I wear jackboots under my overalls.

HAMMER: Nah, you're too foreign looking.

MOLE: Isn't that foreman in Dispatch one?

HAMMER: Ted? Yeah, he used to be. Ferry had a big row with him, he got the push.

MOLE: That's right. Afterwards, Ferry peed all over his locker, said it was his way of saying sorry.

BIRDMAN: They sacked the foreman?

HAMMER: It wasn't for that. He used to read all these Dennis Wheatley books, wasn't it? Yeah, *To the Devil – a Daughter*, *The Satanist*, had hundreds of them. He was very interested in the occult. He became a vampire in the end.

BIRDMAN: Vampire?

HAMMER: Claimed he was. Management said it was all right with them as long as he didn't use his position in the firm to further his own ends.

BIRDMAN: I'd better watch myself around Dispatch then.

HAMMER: Well, that's just it, he didn't. One night he crept along the corridor and sank his teeth into the Works Manager's neck, so they got rid of him.

MOLE: They wouldn't have bothered if he'd bit anybody from the shop floor.

HAMMER: That's the story of our lives.

FERRY *(voice from offstage, then he peers through door)*: Are you still here? *(To* BIRDMAN.*)* I thought you left ages ago. Word's already got out. There's a two-mile queue for your job outside. Didn't fancy Walsall, then?

MOLE: On the stronger stuff now?

FERRY *(warningly to* MOLE*)*: One word!

HAMMER: The T&G wants women stewards, eh?

FERRY: Tough going? Wear a low-cut blouse or a short skirt, that'll attract attention to you.

HAMMER: You never stop, do you, and we're the strongest section.

FERRY: Go and hammer management, that's your job, leave me alone!

HAMMER: Hammer management on my own? You know the stewards have been offered a room in the offices? They've accepted it.

FERRY: Handy for tea and biscuits. Good idea – show you all their problems!

HAMMER: I thought you would have been interested that they're trying to close Linwood, we could be for the chop! All you care about is your job.

FERRY: I've changed my mind, I quite fancy the redundancy money. Crisp £1 notes, I can buy a second-hand Avenger.

HAMMER: Traitor!

FERRY: Me, traitor? Go up and ask those Jocks who are threatening our jobs, They're the traitors, love!

HAMMER: You know what I mean!

BIRDMAN *(to* FERRY*)*: I've been listening to you since I started here!

FERRY: That's nice for you. Fly away, Birdman!

HAMMER: Mole's right. What's the point in bothering with you, eh?

FERRY: Mole?

MOLE: I'll be down my tunnel if anybody wants me! (*MOLE lingers as the temperature rises.*)

HAMMER: If we squeeze a sore we shouldn't be surprised to see the pus running out of it!

FERRY: That's lovely – I hope you negotiate like this!

BIRDMAN: What was all that stuff you gave me about working together?

FERRY: That stands. Well, I do, anyway! I take the splanges off the press, pass them to you, you finish them – okay?

HAMMER: Don't get too close, the pus might splash out and infect you.

FERRY: Oh, we wouldn't want that, would we? I might corrupt the ex-con!

(*BIRDMAN makes a grab at FERRY.*)

FERRY: Fancy me, do you, eh? (*Facing up to him with fists raised.*)

(*BIRDMAN turns away from fight.*)

FERRY: Chicken! I've changed my mind – I think you'll fit very well in here! Join the rest of the brood. Well, thanks for the entertaining break. (*Exits.*)

BIRDMAN: Sorry, I shouldn't have gone for him.

HAMMER: Why apologise to me?

BIRDMAN: Just reacted.

HAMMER: If you think he's bad, wait until you come face to face with management.

MOLE: Ferry's all right, he won't think anything of it.

HAMMER: Look, if you work here long enough it'll twist you. It happens to all of us – it suits them down to the ground! We're playing right into their hands!

BIRDMAN: Where do we go from here, then?

MOLE (*shouts*): There's plenty of room in my tunnel!

(*HAMMER exits.*)

MOLE: What did I say?

BIRDMAN: I don't think it had anything to do with you.

MOLE: They've all gone up here. (*Indicates head.*) Acting as if it's a big surprise, well, they haven't twisted me! It's only a matter of time before Chrysler pulls out – everybody knows that, known it for months.

BIRDMAN: Why did they start me then?

MOLE: I'll be down my tunnel if anyone wants me! (*Exits down tunnel.*)

BIRDMAN (*sitting on square block in front of the lockers, addressing audience*): For a while I shared a cell with an Asian. He was an awkward sod. He couldn't speak any English, so they never let him send any of his letters out. Some rule about their right to censor all mail. He was totally isolated, alone. Tried to talk to him, get through to him, but he never said a word. Most nights he started crying, then shouting. One night, after he'd been in about a month, he went berserk, smashing up the cell. I tried to calm him down but he carried on. They sent for the doctor. He said he was a danger to himself and me and gave him a sedative, starting him on quieteners to help him adjust. The doctor turned to me and asked me if I wanted some. So I told him, 'That's what I'm in here for!' Birdman? No, I won't fly away, Ferry – I've landed here.

(*BIRDMAN is looking out the window, HAMMER and FERRY enter from side.*)

HAMMER: They've gone back to work at Linwood, it's been settled, sent more orders down. It's back to normal.

BIRDMAN: Thank Christ for that!

FERRY: Oh, I doubt if *he* was actually at the negotiating table.

HAMMER: Well, now we're safe we can start on the pay claim.

FERRY: I always said that Linwood would be all right.

BIRDMAN: Yeah!

FERRY: Did they win?

HAMMER: I think so, the supervisors called it off. I suppose they did.

BIRDMAN: I thought you said management provoked them?

HAMMER: From what we heard.

FERRY (*peering over edge of* MOLE'*s hole, then reaching down as if helping* MOLE *up*): Well, we'll probably get the full story in the papers tomorrow, eh?

MOLE (*emerging from his tunnel, breathing hard*): Just a few more feet I reckon, not long at all now!

FERRY: Back to normal.

HAMMER: Right, well, now you're all here, there's trouble next door and they need our help.

BIRDMAN: At the food factory?

FERRY: It's a textile firm.

BIRDMAN: Chemicals.

MOLE: They knit soya.

FERRY: Pyjamas?

MOLE: Pork chops.

HAMMER: At the hospital!

BIRDMAN: That's after you eat them.

HAMMER: Part of the cuts.

MOLE: Pork chops!

HAMMER: The hospital! Look, we've started a petition, there's a collection going around.

FERRY: Tell them they can have a bit of my National Insurance stamp.

HAMMER: I'm going down there this afternoon.

BIRDMAN: We could raise a levy through the Branch.

FERRY *(to HAMMER)*: He's after your job! Raise a levy? We stand more chance of raising Lazarus!

BIRDMAN: We should support them!

FERRY: We'll send Mole over to dig them out!

HAMMER: Back to normal . . .

BIRDMAN *(to FERRY)*: Come on, that's what we're in the union for isn't it?

FERRY: Take Birdman to one side, Hammer.

MOLE: Well, I'm coming up near the morgue in about a week. We can join up with them then.

FERRY: Yeah.

BIRDMAN: I thought you said you were leaving? What's stopping you, then?

FERRY: He's after my job as well!

BIRDMAN: No I'm not, you're always shooting your mouth off, let's hear it, then!

HAMMER: What's the point?

BIRDMAN: Look, I stuck it out with you, I know what it means. (To FERRY.) Why do you stay?

FERRY: Why does anyone stay? Work, the money – we're all in it because of the money!

BIRDMAN: Okay, what does that mean?

FERRY (to MOLE): Have you been giving him lessons? (To BIRDMAN.) Don't you understand cash? I know inside they might give you plastic beads, but here, straight from the government? Money!

BIRDMAN: Yeah, to get your money you need your jobs, so you've got to keep fighting for the job to get your money!

HAMMER: I told you our jobs are safe!

BIRDMAN: I know, but what I'm trying to get through to him is you can't fight on your own. That's why we're in the union.

FERRY: I don't believe I'm hearing this. It's like Playschool for the T&G!

BIRDMAN: Come on, then, why are you in the union?

MOLE: He was in the union ages before you came here.

BIRDMAN: He can't answer! Linwood knew what they were fighting for and all he could do was spew out against them!

HAMMER: There's no argument now, right?

BIRDMAN: Till the next time ...

FERRY: Listen, son, for all your words about the union, you're an innocent. You haven't even begun to understand what it means, either here or anywhere else. Look, I don't know what it was like where you worked before, but here, at the arse end of the Detroit gangsters' empire, the union is a group of old-time militants who in-between swapping tales of their glorious past help plan the rationalisation of all our jobs, the Jocks as well. But you're right, I don't much care for them, but then I don't much care for villain converts to the fraternity and equality brigade either! Surely you're not going to give up the one thing you must have learnt in your brief stay elsewhere – that it's dog eat dog! No – I wasn't always like this, I used to be a convert too. Oh, it's all very complex, and just to complicate matters further, our own union leaders who we the members voted for, when we ask for more money, turn around and try to smash us!

HAMMER: You're right, Ferry, but we're not dogs, not animals – although you come very close to it sometimes. It's because you think we are that you turn on us. But there's only one enemy, and the gangsters are happy to see us tear into ourselves, are happy to keep it that way, in case we turn on them! So they throw us the odd bone to keep us happy, because they think we're animals as well. And all the venom you reserve for us should be for them! You know they're the real enemy, yet – true to the traitor you are – you try to weaken us against Chrysler and all the rest.

FERRY: The shop floor's the same as me!

HAMMER: Why? Because after three years of wage restraint, and the day-to-day blackmailing that it's our fault for crisis after crisis, the shop floor didn't fight for more money – and that left you bitter. It's because we're not animals that the blackmailing had some effect. And you say it's money we're here for. I suppose it is, I agree with you. How else can we survive? But I care about what happens to the hospital next door – and so do other people here too. And I care about Linwood jobs because they work for the same gangster, and it could have been us next. And that's why we need to help. Because they're trying to turn us into animals and they never will. What we have to start trying to do is go back to basics.

BIRDMAN: Where do we begin?

HAMMER: Well, Ferry?

FERRY: I was miles away. I just wondered what you'd look like with no clothes on.

(Fade to black.)

Scene 6

(HAMMER enters hospital and looks around. There is banging coming from the hospital bed again.)

HAMMER *(to audience)*: Looks as if it'll fall down before they pull it down. Ferry . . . at least he keeps me aware of what I'm up against. He's no worse than many of the men are behind your back. He's honest or straightforward enough to say it to your face. You get used to being looked on as a lump of meat. When I'm here they confirm it. Gynaecologists? *(She jumps and turns as if spoken to by figure in hospital bed.)* Hey? Oh, somebody will be along in a minute. *(She takes out a piece of paper and starts to read it.)*

(HOSPITAL PORTER enters, whistling loudly, carrying a bin. He pauses at door, looking at HAMMER, who is oblivious, reading the paper. Eventually she looks up to see him waiting, and eventually takes a step back, out of his way. He puts his bin down where she had been standing.)

HOSPITAL PORTER *(loudly)*: Excuse me, I noticed the petition!

HAMMER: Oh, are you from the Action Committee?

HOSPITAL PORTER: Full of it!

HAMMER: Good, I wanted to meet somebody to have a word. I got this petition from one of your nurses – Sharon?

HOSPITAL PORTER: That's COHSE!

HAMMER: That's nice, I've just spent all afternoon getting this filled in!

HOSPITAL PORTER: No, the union's COHSE, they produce it!

HAMMER: Well, here it is. *(Passing him petition.)* I'm from Solo's next door and we discussed your request for support.

HOSPITAL PORTER *(reading petition)*: Ferry was always very reliable!

HAMMER: Has he been in?

HOSPITAL PORTER: A while ago. I mentioned it to him. Did he meet up with the other stewards? Of course you probably wouldn't know about that.

HAMMER: I'm a steward there. And we did discuss your request for support, yeah.

HOSPITAL PORTER: Really?

HAMMER: Yes. We'd like to help in any way we can. Especially Ferry.

HOSPITAL PORTER: Sounds excellent news, boost to morale! Effluent! We're coming down hard on disposed effluent! We'll be in touch. *(Exits.)*

HAMMER *(to audience)*: It's only an investigation, tests, something to do with my uterus. They drew pictures of it for me, used different colour biros. There's a simple reason why I can't have kids, they said. But they're not too hopeful. They've probed several times. I've got a stack of drawings at home. Some of them are quite pretty.

(Two white-coated men appear, one on either side, and one helps HAMMER into a hospital gown.)

HAMMER: They keep on looking, but they're not that sure what they're investigating for. Just one of those things.

(The men lift HAMMER up and place her upside down, so that her head and arms are dangling towards the audience. They both lift a corner of the hospital gown with her legs in the air, and hold it up so that it forms a screen over her lower torso.)

HAMMER: I'm not the only one. There's plenty more in the same boat. At first I resented being just one of many. Mine seemed to be the least important problem amongst all that it's possible to have done to your body. Abortions. Hysterectomies. But chatting to the other women waiting, as time passed we got to know each other, and our feelings changed. Sharing our fear felt like a strength. There was such bravery too from the least expected people. Some of my results have been encouraging.

(*The two men lower the hospital gown and* HAMMER *sits up. They lift her to her feet, take off the gown, and she turns to face the audience again.*)

HAMMER: If you want something bad enough, or good enough, perhaps you can make it happen. A lot of it's in the mind, you see, a vicious circle. If you believe it can't be done, that affects you. Have faith. If you believe in it, that it's possible, there's a good chance you can make it happen. Have faith, the doctor said, have faith. It doesn't matter so much about the baby now. (*Hears a noise and turns head to speak to body on trolley.*) Hey? Oh, somebody will be along in a minute.

(*Fade to black.*)

Scene 7

(*Back in the Solo Diecast factory.*)

FERRY: A return of free collective bargaining? Who are you kidding? When has it ever been free?

BIRDMAN: We've put in for 15 per cent. Hammer reckons things are looking up.

FERRY: Just a game!

BIRDMAN: Oh, try and be happy will you? It's what you wanted all along!

FERRY: Well, I suppose I could do with the money, but you're forgetting Chrysler's will never break the government's 5 per cent. It'd put their wage freeze in jeopardy!

BIRDMAN: You're never satisfied, are you? Always something wrong!

FERRY: What, being realistic in your fairyland?

BIRDMAN: At the last meeting, the stewards were all for it! Ask anyone on the shop floor!

FERRY: Coming out of the coop? Could be dangerous you know!

BIRDMAN: The sore seems to be healing up. (*He reaches over the painted lathe to help* MOLE *emerge from his tunnel.*)

(MOLE *emerges from tunnel, breathing heavily.*)

MOLE: Tomorrow by the latest. I can hear people moving about overhead. I could've overshot a bit though. I might come up in the morgue.

FERRY: Have you ever thought, Mole, that being so close is the most dangerous time of all?

MOLE: It's safe as a rock down there. A bomb could go off and the roof would stay up.

FERRY: Discovery! There's a very dodgy-looking security guard just started – he's already commented on the collapsed suspension in your Anglia. One word from him and it could start a whole investigation!

MOLE: If you've told anybody anything . . . (*Moves aggressively towards* FERRY.)

FERRY: No.

BIRDMAN: You bloody traitor!

FERRY: I'm telling you – I haven't told anyone, okay?

MOLE: You think you're so clever, don't you? Well, I'm no idiot! Or stupid!

FERRY: I realise that, Mole. O-level Technical Drawing, it's an honour to work with you.

MOLE: You think the thought of betrayal never crossed my mind? I hadn't planned for it? Expected it? That's why I've always had an ace up my sleeve!

FERRY: I was only teasing you, Mole!

MOLE: The first law of escape is, never put all your eggs in one basket! Always have an alternative. (*MOLE moves the lockers to one side and points to the floor.*) Mole's tunnel – Mark II!

(*BIRDMAN peers down into another hole. When FERRY comes over to look, MOLE quickly places the lockers back over the spot.*)

(*Enter HAMMER, reading a newspaper, looking serious.*)

FERRY: Oh, you can tell by the smile on her face that they've given in! What, you didn't stop at an extra £20 a week, you went straight for 35 hours, restored differentials, eh?

BIRDMAN: You all right?

HAMMER (*passing the newspaper to BIRDMAN*): Read for yourself.

FERRY: Chrysler's have changed over to producing life-sized Petula Clarks, and there's not a splange in her!

BIRDMAN (*reading newspaper*): They've sold out!

FERRY: What's new?

BIRDMAN: To Peugeot!

FERRY: Who?

BIRDMAN: Chrysler UK, they've sold the lot, garages, plants, to the French firm!

HAMMER: I'm not sure if we should feel relieved or start panicking again.

FERRY: Peugeot? The French? Don't they make cart-horse trailers?

BIRDMAN: Says here we'll be part of the biggest car manufacturer in Europe!

MOLE: Nice of them to let us know what was going on!

HAMMER: Yeah, well, it does depend on government approval.

FERRY: But the Yanks hate the French!

MOLE: Suppose they are cutting their losses.

HAMMER: It's the government that will have the losses!

BIRDMAN: Says they sold it for £110 million!

FERRY: But to the French?

BIRDMAN: They can hardly sell it to British Leyland.

HAMMER: We could be better off in the long run.

FERRY: I know we've had our problems here, but to sell it to the French?

MOLE: All the best tunnels were dug by the French Resistance during the war!

HAMMER: What does it matter who's bought it?

BIRDMAN: Yeah, it was only ever a gamble for Chrysler.

FERRY: Question is: do cart-horse trailers need splanges?

BIRDMAN: He says it's no threat to the jobs, Peugeot intend to expand their British markets.

HAMMER: Well, it's a good excuse to get all the Chrysler stewards together, anyway.

MOLE: Why didn't they give it to the government? Nationalise it.

FERRY: After all those years of sacrifice for the country.

HAMMER: They're just looking after their own. They'd prefer to sell it to fellow gangsters.

FERRY: I can't see the government allowing it, not after all the money they've sunk in it.

MOLE: I suppose it was cheaper than slinging us on the dole, eh?

HAMMER: And they never said a word to us, not a word.

FERRY *(dejected)*: Lumps of garlic in your wage packet . . .

BIRDMAN: If we're guaranteed jobs we might be better off.

FERRY: I don't know, the French are funny, they *like* work.

HAMMER: Oh come on, I bet it's the same as the shop floor here.

BIRDMAN *(to FERRY)*: So much for getting at Linwood. We're all in the same boat now.

HAMMER: Well, Ferry?

FERRY: All this turmoil, it confuses you.

BIRDMAN: As Hammer says, it's back to basics!

MOLE: I could start on a Channel Tunnel! *(He disappears behind his lathe.)*

HAMMER: We could be safer with Peugeot.

FERRY: The traitors!

BIRDMAN: Chrysler's a multinational!

FERRY: I suppose so. But who are the patriots and traitors now?

HAMMER: We'll have to see!

(Fade to black.)

Scene 8

(FERRY sitting alone, talking to MOLE down in hole.)

FERRY: I didn't realise they owned Citröen's as well. Have you seen them, Mole? They're a good motor. Aerodynamic. Hydraulic suspension. Inside curved, beautiful finish. Just like the Tardis. Gearbox needs five splanges alone. CX! Stands for Citröen Extraordinaire! Well, I thought I'd learn a bit of French, make the new bosses feel at home, you know. Comprenez-vous merde! Hey, what do you think then, Mole? Save up £10 a week, you could have one – for your retirement. Hey, Mole? Mole? *(Gets up, runs over to MOLE's first tunnel and bangs on the lathe, shouting.)* Mole? Mo-o-o-le?

(MOLE rushes onto stage from other side.)

MOLE: They've taken over! Next door! At the hospital! Hammer and Birdman have just come back. The stewards said they want as many people as possible to go over and show support!

FERRY: With the accidents we have here you'd think we give them enough business already!

MOLE: Exciting though, isn't it, taking over the hospital like that.

FERRY: I suppose my next appointment's gone by the board.

MOLE: No, it's business as usual! It's great fun – I'm going back over.

FERRY: What about your tunnel?

MOLE: Oh, I'll finish it tomorrow!

FERRY: Wonders will never cease!

(HAMMER enters.)

HAMMER: The papers are coming down . . .

MOLE: To take photos next door – we should take our T&G banner over.

(BIRDMAN *enters.*)

FERRY: What about the small matter of the French invasion here?

HAMMER: It's all been taken care of. We've got assurances.

BIRDMAN: They dare not try anything, our pay claim will scare them to death!

FERRY: What Napoleon failed to do, eh?

HAMMER: Tragic! Go and man the beaches if you're feeling that threatened. We're going over. Coming, Ferry?

MOLE: Everybody'll be there!

FERRY: My doctor won't! He's probably making a last ditch stand in Outpatients against the red hordes.

MOLE: Why, are they coming as well?

FERRY: Must have been the summer that did it – two weeks stuck at Heathrow Airport is enough to make anyone revolt.

HAMMER: I have to go to the stewards' room. I've got a message to go there urgently. (*Exits.*)

MOLE: It takes a lot of guts to take over.

FERRY: Collapsed during the war though, there's a yellow streak there somewhere.

MOLE: At the hospital?

FERRY: Peugeot! Our new French lords and masters!

MOLE: Listen, I'll just nip down my tunnel for five minutes. Don't go without me, will you?

FERRY: No . . .

BIRDMAN: You should come over, the atmosphere's incredible! Like a shot in the arm.

FERRY: On the hard stuff now, are you?

BIRDMAN: Let's call a truce, Ferry.

FERRY: All right. But if you're honestly telling me we've got anything to learn from that hospital lot, you're mad. Do you know what their basic wage is?

BIRDMAN: It's not about money, they're better organised than us. It's back to basics.

FERRY: So it's come to this, has it? Us, car workers, the big battalions, the T&G, being told how to organise by a load of NUPE boot boys? Everything's moving so fast. *(Stares into distance.)* Did I ever tell you about the old Humber Super Snipe?

(HAMMER enters ashen-faced.)

HAMMER: They've closed us down. They just announced it, at the end of the month. *(Raising her voice.)* Peugeot, they've closed us, probably Linwood too!

BIRDMAN: You're joking!

FERRY: At the end of the month?

BIRDMAN: What about all the assurances?

HAMMER: They said it was inevitable, to secure the survival of jobs in other plants.

BIRDMAN: Sold down the river! Hey, what was all that talk about government assurances, international trade union action?

HAMMER: The management here want to meet us next week to discuss redundancy payments.

FERRY: Do you ever get the feeling this has happened all before?

BIRDMAN: Another gamble they hope will pay off.

FERRY: Everything's moving so fast.

BIRDMAN: What about the other stewards?

HAMMER: Shocked as I am.

BIRDMAN: Right then, we'll start on the shop floor, get The Poet working on the bulletin. We can't let them can't get away with it. They've made a bad mistake with their timing! You know what the feeling is about the pay claim!

HAMMER: But they've closed us! It's the final notice. Peugeot said they're not prepared to negotiate.

FERRY: Seeds of traitors in us all then, love.

HAMMER: What the hell do we do though?

BIRDMAN: Forget negotiations, no more games! Let's take a leaf out of the hospital's book – occupy here!

FERRY: I know this sounds stupid, but how the hell do you think we're going to do that, eh?

BIRDMAN: The only way we find out how to do it is by doing it.

FERRY: Look who's taking the gamble now! It's just ridiculous! Occupy here? We'd be better off taking the money. Most of them would here, too.

HAMMER (*excitedly*): We could take a chance.

BIRDMAN: We've nothing to lose. As we've said, every time we negotiate with management, we play with a loaded dice. And now we've no choice left. If most of us want to keep our jobs – and I think most do – well, let's occupy!

MOLE (*emerges from tunnel, arms outstretched as if in triumph, shouting*): Freedo-o-o-o-m! Freedom! I'm through! I'm out! I'm free! (*Laughs and coughs and splutters.*)

FERRY: How're we going to break it to him?

MOLE: No more than ten feet out, I'm right by the hospital laundry – look! (*Holds up a sign that reads 'Occupied Against Closure'.*) I've brought one of their placards back to prove it!

BIRDMAN: That'll be useful. (*Takes placard from* MOLE.)

FERRY: Come over here, Mole, I want to have a word with you.

(MOLE *approaches and looks curiously at him.* FERRY *turns away.*)

FERRY: I can't do it, you know.

HAMMER: Mole, Peugeot are trying to close us down.

MOLE: Oh, Chrysler – don't worry.

HAMMER: We're going to occupy.

MOLE: Yeah, I told them we're coming straight through, right by the hospital laundry!

FERRY: No, no, no. We're going to occupy here, Mole, Solo Diecast's.

MOLE: Here?

HAMMER: Fighting back. (*Exits.*)

MOLE (*looking plaintively at* FERRY): But I'm through! Out! Free.

FERRY (*puts his arm around* MOLE): I know, Mole. But you're not really, are you? I mean, even if you do leave here, eh, where will you go? Probably on the dole for God knows how long, and even if you do manage to get another job, well – you might not meet people like us, they might not want you digging away at their firm's foundations. I know it's your way of getting your own back, but there is no escape, not unless we all find one together. And if we take over here – well, it's a break with the rules, it'll change the way they see us! Well, frees us from clocking on, eh?

MOLE (*determined*): Seizing your prison's freedom is it?

FERRY (*picks up large block, sits on it and clasps his hands*): Did I ever tell you about the old Humber Super Snipe? You'd have loved that, Mole, you had to get right underneath . . .

(*Fade to black.*)

Scene 9

(Back to the opening scene of their own occupation (Scene 1). HAMMER and BIRDMAN are looking out the window, and FERRY is looking around the room.)

FERRY: Bit of an anti-climax really.

HAMMER and BIRDMAN *(together)*: Shut up!

FERRY: Very successful when you weigh it up, I suppose.

HAMMER: Where's the Mole?

FERRY: Down the hole.

BIRDMAN: If we barricaded that main gate and just used the tunnel, this place would be like a fortress.

HAMMER: It's a great way to get supplies in, keep in contact with the hospital. We can make management crawl through it to hold negotiations.

BIRDMAN: What time did the office say Daley was coming down?

HAMMER: About ten o'clock.

FERRY: Daley! The Union District Official himself! He won't like this you know. He goes to see Manchester City on Saturdays. He's not too bad though. He tried to recruit them all to the union once – he never did. Then they slid right down the division.

HAMMER: Linwood's sending a delegation down.

FERRY: You did that deliberately, didn't you?

BIRDMAN: Granada TV's coming.

FERRY: I suppose we'll end up another millstone of history.

(Banging and coughing from MOLE's tunnel. MOLE emerges, coughing, and hangs over the side of the lathe for a moment.)

FERRY: You know I knew this would happen, he's got Mole's Lung.

MOLE (*taking out papers and holding them in front of* HAMMER *and* BIRDMAN): The Poet's just finished his bulletins. He said he's going to the Trades Council tonight and he wants four or five people to go around the factories.

FERRY: I'm amazed how we ever managed to pull this off. It just shows you, doesn't it, eh?

HAMMER: People must be wondering what was happening, what with the hospital occupation and now us. If Linwood joins us . . .

BIRDMAN: What will Peugeot do?

FERRY: I bet they're panicking. They've only got another 150,000 working for them . . .

HAMMER: Not still trying to bring us down, are you?

MOLE (*moving to centre stage with arms outstretched*): Listen! A moat, 4-foot wide!

FERRY: A moat, Mole, is a mistake. We've got enough defences with your tunnel already.

MOLE: 3-foot wide then! (*He exits.*)

(*All are reading the bulletins.*)

HAMMER: Look at the other factories The Poet's got supporting us! He's amazing!

BIRDMAN: Seems the old guard isn't dead yet then!

FERRY: I've always said that. They've got a lot of experience, the old ones.

HAMMER: Did you see the back of the bulletin?

FERRY: Wei Lin Chinese Takeaway?

BIRDMAN: How'd he ever get adverts for the occupation bulletin?

HAMMER: No, underneath that.

BIRDMAN: It's a poem.

FERRY: 'Partisans'?

HAMMER: 'Joy with struggle . . .'

FERRY: Which girl's Joy then?

HAMMER *(reading poem)*: 'Joy with struggle is our highest goal, and to fight as one, strength with strength, in knowing together we shall be all. So don't fear enemies who choose to pawn their reason for ignorance. They'll never try to command our spirit, only try to crush its vital force, each one of us a victim.'

FERRY: What a summer.

BIRDMAN: At least we can look forward to a warm winter.

HAMMER: I think we should paint that on the wall outside, eh? Joy with Struggle!

BIRDMAN: Come on, let's have that dance. Joy with Struggle!

HAMMER: Joy with Struggle!

*(*HAMMER *and* BIRDMAN *link hands as if about to waltz, and exit stage.)*

FERRY: I know struggle. But who's this Joy?

*(*FERRY *holds up placard that says 'THE END'.)*

(Fade to black.)